ENDS
&
BEGINNINGS

CITY LIGHTS REVIEW #6

Edited by

Lawrence Ferlinghetti

Front cover: Mimmo Paladino. *Senza Titolo*, (bronze & iron), 1993.
Courtesy Mimmo Paladino.
Cover design: John Miller, Big Fish Books

ISBN: 0-82786-292-5
ISSN: 1045-1943

City Lights Books are available to bookstores through our primary
distributor: Subterranean Company, P.O. Box 160, 265 S. 5th St.,
Monroe, OR 97456. 503-847-5274. Toll-free orders 800-274-7826.
FAX 503-847-6018. Our books are also available through library
jobbers and regional distributors. For personal orders and catalogs,
please write to City Lights Books, 261 Columbus Avenue,
San Francisco, CA 94133.

CITY LIGHTS BOOKS are edited by Lawrence Ferlinghetti and
Nancy J. Peters and published at the City Lights Bookstore,
261 Columbus Avenue, San Francisco, CA 94133.

CONTENTS

DOCUMENTS:

The EDITOR'S unEASY CHAIR

It's *fin du siècle* again, and most everything in this issue is an end or a beginning. There are many looks backward and many forward, sometimes in close conjunction with each other. There is the discovery of America and the discovery of Chiapas on the revolutionary map of today. There is the conjunction of disparate generations in the meeting of confused Confucian Ezra Pound and the anti-fascist Pier Paolo Pasolini (an interview never before published in full in English). And there is a literary scoop of sorts in the conjunction of D.H. Lawrence's Sunday paintings and the Elgin Marbles. We see old USSR through its birds, we see the 'end' of racism from a Chicago retrospect and its perpetual embodiment in possible Hitlers of the future. Among other unpublished literary news, there is Rimbaud's letter written in English to the American Navy and an ad for a sure way to exterminate yuppies. And there are numerous poets radically different from each other, some gazing backward, some into a visionary future.

There also is art by Dario Fo and the famous Italian painter Mimmo Paladino.

The Editor's Chair is obviously on a swivel, a wide-angle vision being a necessity these violent days, seated as he is on the left side of a world about to implode into the 21st century in which migrant populations in search of food and shelter may sweep the earth, and nations as we know them no longer exist.

— *Lawrence Ferlinghetti*

Dario Fo　　Photograph by Paolo Calzà

JOHAN PADAN DISCOVERS THE AMERICAS

A Scene from a Play by

DARIO FO

with illustrations by the Author

Once the Spanish conquistadores were escorted to their ship by the Indios, I called a meeting of all the chiefs, caciques, lieutenant caciques, shamans, the leaders of the elders and the leaders of the women. These people represented something like fifteen different tribes, the five thousand people who had followed us there.

So I made this speech to them: "Listen good folks, the time will come we'll run into a large army of Christian forces, and their governor. You can't escape from these wicked people forever. There's only one way to stick it to them. We're going to take away the pretext they've been using to enslave you and kill you, and that's the fact that you're not Christians. So I'll turn you into Christians! Yes, Christian-Infidel Indians."

"And how are you going to do that?"

"Easy. You just need someone to teach you catechism. And I'm sorry to say I'm the only one here qualified for that! So everybody sit down, and I'll start our first lesson."

All the Indios, men, women, thousands of them, gathered around me.

"Rule number one," I begin, "you've got to know that in this

Catholic religion of ours, once you die it's not completely over. What happens is that those who were good while they were alive go to heaven and those who were really bad go to hell."

"Excuse me," they ask, "and those Spanish Christians we just ran into — they're going to heaven too?"

"Yes, if they repent of their sins before they die."

"Well, if those people are going to heaven, then we'd rather go to hell!"

Ah, we're really off to a good start here!

So, anyway, I start telling them about the Creation, about Adam and Eve, about God the Father. The story about the big scoundrel serpent who wanted to get Eve to eat the apple was very well received. But then a problem came up about the apple, 'cause in the Indies there are no apples — they've never even seen them — so I substituted a mango. And the Indios weren't at all happy with this mango thing: "It's not right that this god should forbid mangoes! Mangoes are the fruit we like best. I'd have eaten that scoundrel serpent instead. I've have eaten the whole thing raw!"

It was useless to try to get them to understand the little detail about modesty, that it was a strange thing for Adam and Eve to go around naked. The idea of covering yourself — they couldn't get that into their heads. Cover yourself up? Hide your shame? And with a fig leaf at that! They've never seen our fig leaves — the closest thing they've got is the Indies fig — the cactus — full of thorns — and you've got to put it right *there*?! Right over your *bergonzoli*? Ah, what fun!

It was hard to discuss these things with them. And you should see how mad they got when I told them about the Angel of God, who came down with his sword of fire to throw Adam and Eve out of the Garden of Eden. They all shouted: "That angel must have been one of those Spanish bastards!"

Then they asked me: "What was the garden of Eden like, that paradise they were thrown out of?"

"Well it was a land as sweet and beautiful as this one."

"So God didn't throw us out, since we are still living in the very same place!"

They were right.

But the most difficult problem was getting them to accept the

DARIO FO   3

mystery of the Trinity. The Father, that's ok. The Son, that's fine too, actually they liked him right away. But what they really couldn't stomach was this thing about the Holy Ghost being a pigeon. "'Cause pigeons are really disgusting. It's a crazy animal — pushy as hell. If a pigeon runs into another bird who's in trouble, even if it's the same species, wham! he jumps him and pecks him to death like a coward! It eats the eggs from other birds' nests — and above all, it's got the bad habit of shitting everywhere, even while it's flying! Splat! And, then, it's always full of fleas, ticks — and it carries diseases. No, no, you can't put a pigeon in the holy Trinity."

Ok, so instead we put in the Virgin Mary, and she really did fit a lot better.

Another character they couldn't figure out at all was St. Joseph. They liked him a lot but they couldn't swallow the fact that he was just the father as a figure of speech, not for real. But what really didn't go down well was that he was supposed to sleep by himself in a hammock, and not with the Virgin Mary, and that he was always kept on one side of the manger with the ox and the donkey, keeping the place warm with his breath. What a weird family!

Now, the character who met with immediate success was Mary Magdalene. When I introduced her as a real good-looking woman, lusty and passionate, they all started clapping.

Riding the wave of their enthusiasm, without even thinking it through, I began the story about her, the adulteress, Mary Magdalene, thrown against a pillar, half naked, and surrounded by a crowd of fanatics ready to throw stones.

Good thing, in the nick of time I had Jesus arrive on the scene and shout: "That's enough, stop it! Let he who is without sin cast the first stone! And you, mamma, put that rock down, it's none of your affair."

Mary Magdalene, naked as she was, at the height of emotion starts to faint. He, Jesus, takes her in his arms, sweeps her onto his horse — 'cause he was always on his horse — and whee, off they go.

But it was really impossible to field all the questions they kept shooting at me: "Excuse me, Mr. holy man, so was Mary Magdalene really Jesus' lover?"

"I think so, but I'm not sure."

"What do you mean, you're not sure? The two of them slept in the same hammock, right?"

"I think so, maybe they did."

"So they made love?"

"That, I don't know."

"What do you mean, 'I don't know'?" This lusty Mary Magdalene had been with lots of men. She really liked to get it on, so do you think that all she did with the Son of God was swing in the hammock to keep cool? They did make love, didn't they?

"Yeah, maybe they were in love."

"And maybe she got pregnant? How many times?"

"No, I don't think so."

"What do you mean, you don't think so? She didn't have any children?"

"Well, maybe — but the Gospels don't say that."

"They sure must have ripped out those pages, where Mary Magdalene was always pregnant by Jesus! That's why Jesus said: 'Suffer the little children come unto me. . . .' You think he just meant other people's kids? I say, I bet a lot of those kids were his!"

And about the Apostles? All male, not a single female? That one deserved some investigation. So I had to patch it up a little: half of them for sure were male, and the other six were Apostelettes! One Apostelette, for example, was named Joan, another Paula, another Mattea. And then, it turned out that these twelve Apostles walked two by two, arm in arm, males with females, and they really loved one another. Judas was the only one who didn't have a female counterpart — and that's why he became a betrayer.

These Indios then were crazy about miracle stories, but I had to work on them a bit so they'd add up. For example, the wedding feast in Cana. I couldn't tell them about the miracle of the water turning into wine — there's no wine in the Indies — there's palm beer or cactus beer. And then you couldn't turn water into beer in one fell swoop! The fact is that Indios never drink water at a banquet, they drink goats' milk. So when they say: "Master, we're stuck without a drop of beer left," he doesn't tell them: "Bring me a dozen jugs of milk," but, "Bring me twelve goats with nice full udders." These goats, appear, the Son of God lifts three fingers and blesses the udders and says, "Now, try to milk them. And, ah, a miracle! From the goats, tiddies out comes chic — chic — cactus beer, wonderfully cool and foamy! And they all get drunk like gods! Ha!

But when I came to tell them about Jesus being betrayed by Judas, arrested, about the trial and the sentence, they were listening without even daring to breathe.

Even worse was when I started telling about the cross, about the nails being driven into his flesh, about his mother at the foot of that cross, tearing out her heart watching him die. They all started crying desperately, just as though one of their own children had died! And they scratched their faces, tore out their hair.

"Calm down — it happened so many years ago!" But there was no way, they just wouldn't quiet down. They continued to moan and cry their hearts out.

"Cruel and wicked God," they cried, "When your son called you — 'Father, help me!' — why did you do nothing but stay up there playing your guitar with the angels! You let him croak alone, like a dog!"

And so, howling wildly, they threw rocks up at heaven, trying to hit him!

Fortunately, all of a sudden I remembered the resurrection: "Calm down, listen to me: after three days in the grave, Jesus thought it over and came back resurrected."

"No, no, it's not true. You just made up this lie about the resurrection to make us feel better. We don't believe you."

"You don't believe me? The holy man! Look out, 'cause he had an Apostle, Thomas, who didn't believe either, just like you. And he went to check it out for himself, the unbeliever, he went to touch Jesus' wounds as he came out of the tomb — zap! a bold of lightning got him — right on his hands. So he was left with his fingers burnt to the elbow!"

This story about the burnt hands and fingers made a big impression.

"Then it's true that Jesus came back to life! So Christ is still in this world! Hip, hip, hooray!" And they started celebrating in a big way; they began to dance, shout, laugh like crazy! They hugged, made love, drank until they were smashed.

And using a small tube they'd shoot a white powder into each other's nostrils, the pollen of a flower they called *boracero*. One would put this pea-shooter in a friend's nose and then he'd blow very hard and wham! The friend would get high, totally stoned!

"Come on, I can understand your joy about the resurrection, but this is not the proper way to celebrate the Christian Easter! Shame on you! Doing drugs, getting drunk — it's not Christian. And then, making love while you're praying, come on! And cut out all that dancing!"

"Are you saying that Christians don't dance?" they asked me in total amazement.

"No, they're always serious."

"And when they pray, they don't make love?"

"No, never!"

"And they don't drink?

"Only the priest drinks, everybody else just watches."

"Those guys don't drink, don't dance — Christians are always serious, they don't even shoot one another in the nose with the *boracero*. They don't make love when they pray! What kind of a death religion is this?!"

After that, they didn't want to hear one more word about catechism.

Translated by Pina Piccolo & Nancy J. Peters

Dario Fo   Photograph by Corrado Maria Falsini

SUBCOMANDANTE MARCOS

Communiqué

*Excerpt from the communiqué of the Zapatista Army for National
Liberation, issued upon the assassination of PRI presidential candidate,
Luis Donaldo Colosio*

For those whom no one sees:

Greetings, brother zapatista-moles. We have shone, thanks to
your patient work in obscurity. The black night of infamy comes
again. The end of our time is near. We promise you that we will shine
intensely, outdo the sun, before disappearing forever. Until the last
hour, we salute the dark side that supported our brilliance. Hidden
light that shone through us to illumine this small piece of history.

We will be in the front lines, like those who came before us.
We will honor the dignity of our dead. . . . Brother moles, the end of
our road is almost here. It will be your turn then, dear moles. Don't
forget our passing. We were sincere in seeking a window for our fee-
ble light. Learn from this sad story.

Never forget the demand that made us great, even if only for
a moment: Everything for everyone, nothing just for us.

Goodbye, beloved moles, make ready your flag and prepare
those who will have to come after you. The time is coming for you to
cover your face, erase your name, give up your past, nurture your tender fury, and look after your weapons because peace is fleeing as
quickly as it came. Allow us to send you a last greeting, left hand to
the forehead and, also . . .

A Gift and a Political Lesson

A small piece of the moon.
Really it isn't one,
but two little pieces:
A piece of the dark side of the moon
and a piece of the bright side.
And what should be understood
is that the piece of the moon that shines
shines because the dark side exists.
It is the dark side
that makes the bright side
possible. It's the same for us,
if it's our destiny to be the dark side of the moon
we are not less for it,
rather, it's because we are willing
to be the dark side
that it's possible for everyone to see the moon
(and, in the end,
the dark side is more,
because it shines for other skies
and in order to see it
one must learn to fly very high).
And so it is
that few are willing
to suffer so that others will not,
and to die
so that others may live.

And that's the way it is
given boots, and the moon, and etcetera,
and the end.

Well, everlasting moles, we'll meet again underground . . .

Translated by Elaine Katzenberger

WHO IS
SUBCOMANDANTE MARCOS?

When asked whether Subcomandante Marcos, the spokesman for the Zapatistas in Chiapas, was gay, the official communiqué responded:

"Marcos is gay in San Francisco, Black in South Africa, an Asian in Europe, a Chicano in San Ysidro, an anarchist in Spain, a Palestinian in Israel, a Mayan Indian in the streets of San Cristobal, a gang member in Neza, a rocker in the National University, a Jew in Germany, an ombudsman in the Defense Ministry, a communist in the post–Cold war era, an artist without gallery or portfolio . . . , a pacifist in Bosnia, a housewife alone on a Saturday night in any neighborhood in any city in Mexico, a striker in the CTM, a reporter writing filler stories for the back pages, a single woman on the metro at 10 p.m., a peasant without land, an unemployed worker . . . , a dissident amid free-market economics, a writer without books or readers, and of course, a Zapatista in the mountains of southeast Mexico.

"So Marcos is a human being. Any human being in this world.

"Marcos is all the exploited, marginalized, and oppresssed minorities, resisting and saying, 'Enough!'"

Mimmo Paladino   Drawing

ANDREW SCHELLING

OLD AND NEW LITIGATION SONGS

We are danzling on the age of a volcano.
— Finnegans Wake

About three weeks ago the first truckload of contaminated matter left Rocky Flats — first gesture in a decades long clean-up. For local residents this seems good news. But this is not the end of the story, hardly even a beginning. No human mind can grasp the stretch of time through which plutonium, most noxious of known substances, has to be safely stored. The half life of plutonium is 25,000 years.

The truck that transported material out of Boulder County didn't even touch the tons of plutonium stuffed into leaky containers in the compounds at Rocky Flats. By comparison it carried pretty innocuous cargo — laboratory equipment, clothing, boots, office supplies — all mildly contaminated or dusted with radioactive waste. This stuff will be stored underground or more likely incinerated. It doesn't seem to be "our" garbage and of course everyone around here's glad to be rid of it. But wherever the many future truckloads take the waste, into the neighborhoods of people forced, bribed or duped into accepting it, it is not "their" garbage either.

Some quotes from this past Eco-Poetics week —

"The wounded plant and animal species." — *Ed Sanders*
"A hundred species a day die from the planet. Most have no
    name." — *Peter Warshall*
"The end of Nature." — *Anne Waldman*
"Ecocide and ethnocide go hand in hand." — *Diana Hadley*

It has taken a while for it to become apparent that our unprecedented wastage of plant and animal species is either preceded or goes "hand in hand" with the devastation or banishment of human beings. There are, after all, virtually no uninhabited sectors of land on the planet. Whatever the terrain underfoot some human tribe has always found a way to cohabit with other native species — mammals, birds, fish, herbs, trees, waters, and what Peter Warshall calls "the microbial beast" — soil.

Places on earth which have gone untouched by massive extraction of resources, but are now confronting this sort of "harvest," are inhabited by tribal peoples represented to the world community by no government. A decade ago savvy cultural survivalists were calling them "Fourth World" peoples, to distinguish them from Third World governments intent on headlong economic development.

A few truisms that have come to light in recent years —

In order to take the land you have to get rid of the people who live there.
Tribal peoples across the planet are unlikely to live out the decade.

Interesting — just as the preservation or sale of old growth forest in the Pacific Northwest hinges on the "rights" of the spotted owl, or the confrontation over Mt. Graham in Arizona centered on "rights" of the resident Mount Graham red squirrel — so in many beleaguered regions does the battle line get drawn by or around native peoples. Organizations like Cultural Survival and Rainforest Action Network recognized this years ago and saw that the most powerful opposition groups could be, even *had to be*, the human residents of a region.

Much of the world is still in fact tribal. This gets masked because so many tribal peoples, probably the majority that made it into this century as intact tribes, have been displaced from their land — their economic and cultural base. This tears away from them their most identifiable cultural traits, which depend largely on centuries of intimacy with crops, animal neighbors, sacred locales, and artifacts contrived from locally gathered materials — stone, feather, mineral, plant fiber, wood, animal carcass. To displace people from their land is not just to deprive them of real estate. It takes their food, their clothes, their songs, their philosophies. It makes them into *pretas* — hungry homeless ghosts.

Ten years ago when concerned people went around warning of something they called "monoculture," it seemed to mean a world in which everyone ate the same hamburger, watched the same t.v.

show, wore the same clothes, drove the same car. This was a crazy myopia of the wealthy. Nevertheless, it held a seed of truth — the nearly utter loss of this planet's tribal inhabitants. The real monoculture of today's planet has become the dispossessed refugee. The person with no regular food, no t.v., no car. No house, nearly no clothing. The human planetary community no longer recognizes what anthropologist Paul Radin called "the law of the irreducible minimum" — the recognition among aboriginal peoples that every person, simply through membership in the tribe, deserves food, shelter, clothing, companionship. The minimum without which a person can't live.

This was anarchist Peter Kropotkin's critique of Marxism. Marxism had said: *from each according to his ability, to each according to his need.* Kropotkin said no — in a truly human community only the second part of the formula holds. To each according to his or her need. That is enough. The model he gave was that of the public library. When you go into a library, whoever you are you receive the book, the cultural lore, you are after. The librarian doesn't ask if you have a job, if you've swept the walk or cleaned the dishes. That is not the librarian's business, to check up on your work habits. Kropotkin had spent years in his youth living in close proximity to indiginous peoples in Siberia. Later, influenced by Swiss anarchists, he came to believe that this irreducible minimum should be extended across all borders to include the planetary community.

The self-inflicted wounds of the human race.
— *John Daido Loori*

The eight million Afghanees in Pakistan and Iran, the Kurds shuttled back and forth across the borders of Turkey, Iraq and Iran; the shantytown residents of Mexico City and Bombay; Sudanese and Eritrean children, the call girls of Bangkok — these are all tribal peoples. They are being daily reduced to a single indiscriminate mass. The raw materials from which they draw down a livelihood are no longer the produce of ancestral lands, but the refuse of developed nations.

What to do? What to do as writers?

"Become a scholar in chaos." — *Ed Sanders*

"I have an agenda. I am an anarchist. Everything I write is intended to bring about the collapse of Capitalism."
— *Peter Lamborn Wilson*

These words and gestures give a context to writing. Poetry, essay, fiction — activities founded on language use and scholarship. I become firmer and firmer in my belief that restricting yourself to a single literary genre is to be old-fashioned, expectable, possibly irrelevant. Be fluid, athletic, mutable, slippery, unpredictable. You need to. Cries of anguish are rising from every direction.

The person entrusted since ancient times with redressing personal, ecological or social imbalance was the shaman. Song, music, dance, costume comprised the shamanic tools — a secret cultural lore of spirits made up his or her lineage. Historically more recent healers have devised sophisticated poems, novels, essays — the legacy of several thousand years of literacy. Are these enough? Given the urgency, the impending forever loss of peoples and plant and animal species, our planet may now have to add to these a new range of language skills.

Old and new litigation songs.

Learn the songs and stories of the human tribes — life won't mean much in their absence. But there is more — a further imperative we're facing today. This has to do with areas of speech, writing and thought not previously thought of as literary. Law for instance. Investigative journalism's another. Dry as they are, they may point to the mortal underbelly of the Beast. Song is always one of the Beast's unprotected spots, as is humor. But information, compassionate law, precise uses of language may get there equally fast. The Beast protects its tender organs with a webbing of fraudulent language and simulated images. Can you find that soft underbelly and pierce it with an arrow? What are the effective arrows? Are they as they used to be — songs and poems? Sometimes. At moments I think there exist other charms, new weapons, ones we're just beginning to get a grip on. These include lawroom intricacies, revisioned histories, informational newsletters, archival retrieval. Letter writing campaigns. Each of them have stung the Beast. Can you hear the music?

We are writers — men and women of letters. If that means anything it means we inhabit a language-body, the shape of which shifts at the twist of the pen or the closing down of a vowel. With access to this power, why restrict yourself to a single genre? I mean if you don't want arrows and beasts — take bulldozers and monkey-wrenches. In our language-bodies we need to become effective monkeywrenchers.

I've defined monkeywrenching this way: *"Preemptive acts that disable the machinery of destruction."*

Heroes of the Sea Shepherds and Earth First! have led the way here. Quieter citizens also do tough work. For a few months I've been chewing over a phrase — I'd like to link it up with Ed Sanders' "Become a scholar in chaos." *Paper monkeywrenching.* It's a term of derision applied by wilderness warriors towards those who — well, they say there are two types of environmental activists — those who do, and those who do mailings.

From one perspective the division's certainly true. There's some humor here, also a big dose of machismo. I think it's possible to come up with an effective notion of paper monkeywrenching. Paperwork, the tactical application of written language, can disable machinery — because most of the behind-the-scenes machinery is also built of paperwork. Strategies include learning the dance of legal terms and arguments, the unburying of historical truth from libraries, the recovery of suppressed heroic deeds, investigative poetics. These may not replace guerrilla tactics like monkeywrenching hardware in certain flashpoint situations — they're certainly less glamorous — but they bring to bear a different power. A good piece of legislation will stop the bulldozers as surely as a pair of wire clippers.

We should be singing ballads about the law courts! Journalism with the elegance of poetics! At that point poems and stories can pass beyond Elegy — farewell cards to vanishing cultures and extinguished animal species — and move on to a world that takes seriously the law of the irreducible minimum.

"This is the end of the Great Dying."   — *Peter Warshall*
"No Native American language has a word for goodbye."
                                    — *Paula Gunn Allen*

From a talk given at The Naropa Institute, July 4, 1992.

ANNE WALDMAN

MUSE

I am this one writing to be more herself in the thought that all
poems are invented by women. The night or nights of travel being a
shaman of no particular society male or otherwise get spoken exactly
like a love affair and are held as words. As words, these toward the
beloved woman, get mouthed, & she & I, or you & I or She & you
come into being. It is my privilege to speak thus, it is my joy. The
words are an event of no small passion and are forced from a place
outside travel outside time. They arrive here too. And travel was the
name & opportunity of the song as I was always a scribe & sidekick
to her motion. She was my fixed star for a time of heart & I was
perpetual motion too. I catch her as best I can/could through
scent & ambiguity of verse. The pronouns you find in us in here
are a relationship to secret notebooks and hallucinated masks. A
relationship to a web of emptiness dotted with long molecules held
near one another by the action of invisible forces. As forces were
unified only for the smallest fraction of a second at the "beginning
of time," so we both existed and exist that way in words. The "shes"
in it are our relationship. I am the mother most frequently & she
too. And we are both daughters standing between the lines. And
as children we both put on the shields like Amazons. O Sappho!
I want to dance most of the time like a war dance. I feel the
manifestation of speech like an ancient one. I always hear coming
back to me through many lifetimes, what a life to write of adoring
her. Of adoring Her. Now is the chance.

The muse is always my opposite & opposing sister-singer. She is
dark. I am simple. And light. She is not olive, but more a grey like
coal beheld in a dream. She says that she is at the poem's service. To
be loved & stripped & goaded & adored. Questioned, berated. She
is somewhere to put verbs the poet bows down to taste these things
of. Play & scorn. She is a semi-religious figure. Muse is brought

everywhere to life when I chide her. That's the rub or night & day, the two of us. The chide that she not evanesce, that she never cease being difficult is the arising of the connection of power.

Written between edges of the scheme of particular peculiar parameters, the poems of her are of marrow made. The Muse is in marrow of me. The marrow made me a writer. So I write of her for that connection to first Mother-poem that carried in marrow. And was food & light & meat. I extend from here my first syllable "ma." It resides in the heart to be unlocked, to please the mother who talks inside me. All the manifestations of her: bitter sea. The taste of sea & sex & earth. As if you are in her cave. You've been there countless years. You live inside a circle of her words.

You came to Scandinavia to hold your own light. Trees live on every sidewalk. Mountain & sea & Fjord, & here was a land you recognized. Not a pseudonym underneath it. You were holding the light as it stayed at night. You could be illumined in your cave because you held the light of words. Sweet recognition of a point of tongue-origin barbed with love. She is a successful Muse & what legacy can only be approximated here. The Nordic goddesses descend in their teaching mode to instruct on the building of ships & shrines. Give me the wood again, they say.

Who reaps the joy of Muse in the sensual realm? She creates the motive to leap in words the love of our female bodies. Is she that hip? The line is drawn between words of dignity & those that do not further the gender cause. Light up. Light up. I am one of those of the *domos* of Sappho surely. And the cry of sister, sister, I know your sandals because I wear them too. Show me your parts. Who is she? The same age, the same build (a little smaller), size 8 or 10. She is the musk your dreams are made of. She is the terrible secret. She is enfant, Muse terrible. The lady that commands you acknowledge her above all else. And why don't I ever "get" it? To call her sister was always the call. I lighted on her plan to me as a confidant makes. She was not impressed. Muse won't let the drive run. She conquers me.

The poems & how they'd form were always inside me, far back. I needed her as vehicle more than any father, rather to do battle. It's light out the window, 2 a.m. Goddesses walk the light sky. They tell me to keep the story up. They instruct a woman who was slumbering these long centuries to meet you.

Muse was a city. Muse was a road. Muse is my 21st century. For me she was a first civilization. She held me in primal arms, a child in patriarchal ruins. No she goes back further. No she goes forward further. Muse has arms like mine. Muse has my eyes, slightly aslant. Muse's wrists grow cold at night as mine do. Muse sweeps her hair to one side. Muse colors her hair with the clay of Morocco. Muse's legs are pillars of exactitude & exertion. Muse holds her own torso of immense proportion. Muse was born under a sign of water & fire. Her sister Muse is the Bull-Headed-Woman. Muse crawled on her belly once. Muse never humbled herself before the guys. She stole fire back from the father. Muse took the fire and saw herself dancing in there, and the flames were the notes of my songs.

ALLEN GINSBERG

C'mon Pigs of Western Civilization Eat More Grease

Eat Eat more marbled Sirloin more Pork'n gravy!
Lard up the dressing, fry chicken in boiling oil
Carry it dribbling to gray climes, snowed with salt,
Little lambs covered with mint roast in racks surrounded by roast
    potatoes wet with buttersauce,
Buttered veal medallions in creamy saliva, buttered beef, by
    glistening mountains of french fries
Stroganoffs in white hot sour cream, chops soaked in olive oil,
surrounded by olives, salty feta cheese, followed by Roquefort &
    Bleu & Stilton thirsty
for wine, beer Coca-Cola Fanta Champagne Pepsi retsina arak
    whiskey vodka
Agh! Watch out heart attack, pop some angina pills
order a plate of Bratwurst, fried frankfurters,
couple billion Wimpys', McDonald burgers to the moon & burp!
Salt on those fries! Boil onions & breaded mushrooms even zucchini
    in deep hot Crisco pans
Turkeys die only once, look nice next to tall white glasses sugarmilk
    & icecream vanilla balls
Strawberry for sweeter color milkshakes with hot dogs
Forget greenbeans, everyday a few carrots, a mini big spoonful of
    salty rice'll do, make the plate pretty;
throw in some vinegar pickles, briny sauerkraut check yr cholesterol,
    swallow a pill
and order a sugar Cream donut, pack 2 under the size 44 belt
Pass out in the vomitorium come back cough up strands of
    sandwich still chewing pastrami at Katz's delicatessen

Back to Central Europe & gobble Kielbasa in Lódź
swallow salami in Munich with beer, Liverwurst on pumpernickel in
    Berlin, greasy cheese in a 3-star Hotel near Syntagma, on white
    bread thick-buttered
Set an example for developing nations, salt, sugar, fat, coffee
    tobacco Schnapps
Drop dead faster! make room for Chinese guestworkers with alien
    soybean curds green cabbage & rice!
Africans Latins with rice beans & calabash can stay thin & crowd in
    apartments for working class foodfreaks —

Not like Western cuisine rich in protein cancer heart attack
    hypertension sweat bloated liver & spleen megaly
Diabetes & stroke — monuments to carnivorous civilizations
try murdering Belfast Bosnia Cypress Ngorno Karabach Georgia
or mailing love letter bombs in Vienna or setting houses afire in East
    Germany — have another coffee, here's a cigar.
And this is a plate of Black Forest chocolate cake, you deserve it.

Athens, 19 December 1993

Excrement

Everybody excretes different loads
To think of it —
Marilyn Monroe's pretty buttocks,
            Eleanor Roosevelt's bloomers dropt
      Rudolf Valentino on the seat, taut
                  muscles relaxing
Presidents looking down the bowl
                  to see their state of health
our White House rosy-cheeked dieter,
            one last, gaunt sourpuss
                  striped pants ankle'd
                        in the Water Chamber

Name it? by product of
            vegetables, steak, sausages, rice
      reduce to a brown loaf in the watery tureen,
                  splatter of dark mud on highway
                  side cornfields
      studded with peanuts & grape seeds —

Who doesn't attend to her business
No matter nobility, Hollywood starshine, media
            Blitz-heroics, everyone at
                  table follows watercloset
                        regulation & relief
An empty feeling going back to banquet,
            returned to bed, sitting for Breakfast,
      a pile of dirt unloaded from gut level
                  mid-belly, down thru the butthole
                        relaxed & released from the ton
                              of old earth, poured back
                                    on Earth

It never appears in public
        'cept cartoons, filthy canards,
                political comix left & right
the Eminent Cardinal his robes pushed aside,
        Empress of Japan her 60 pound kimono,
                layered silks pushed aside,
the noble German Statesman giving his heart ease
        the pretty student boy in Heidelberg
                between chemic processer abstractions,
        keypunch operators in vast newsrooms
                        Editors their wives and children
                with feces of various colors
                        black with iron supplement
                        to pale green-white sausage
                                delicacies in the same
                                tiny bathroom
                                in distant suburbs,
        even their dogs on green front lawns
                        produce a simulacra of
                        the human garbage
                        we all drop
Myself the Poet ageing on the stool
        Polyhymnia the Muse herself, lowered to this throne —
                what a relief!

                                        3/24/94

WILLIAM S. BURROUGHS

Part of a Telephone Call from Lawrence, Kansas, To NYU Beat Conference at Town Hall, N.Y.C.

I wish the best to each and every one of you, and to quote a fellow Missourian, "Rumors of my demise have been grossly exaggerated." I am in quite good health, though the reason I couldn't come was because my cats need me. I'm sorry.

Now, here's something about Kerouac — my relations with Kerouac.

Kerouac was a writer, that is to say, he wrote. Many people who call themselves writers and have their names on books are not writers, and they do not write. The difference between a bullfighter who fights a bull is different from a bullshitter who makes passes with no bull there. A writer's been there or he can't write about it.

Fitzgerald wrote *The Jazz Age*. "All the sad young men, firefly evenings, winter dreams." He wrote it and brought it back for a generation to read, but he never found his own way back. A whole migrant generation rose from *On The Road* to San Francisco, Mexico, Tangiers, Katmandu.

Novelists are trying to create a universe in which they have lived or where they would like to live. In order to write it, they must go there and submit to conditions which they may not have bargained for. Sometimes, as in the case of Kerouac and Fitzgerald, the effect produced by a writer is immediate, as if a generation were waiting to be written. In other cases, there may be a time lag. Science fiction has a way of coming through fifty years later. By writing a universe, a writer makes such a universe possible.

How useful it is for a writer to act out his own writing in so-called "real life" is an open question. Is he vitalizing his characters and sets by insisting that they be real? Is he taking over reality with his characters and his sets?

In *Winner Take Nothing*, for example, Hemingway's determination to act out the least interesting aspects of his own writing and to actually *be* his main character was, I feel, unfortunate for his writing. If a writer insists on being able to do and do well what his characters do, he limits the range of his characters.

In my own experience, it has been sufficient to do something badly. For example, I was, for one long week — it brings on my ulcers to think about it — a very bad assistant pickpocket. I decided that a week was enough, and turned in my copy of *The Times*. I used to cover the sailor when he put the hand out, and we always used the same copy. He said people would try to read it and get confused when it was months old, and this would keep them from seeing what we were doing. He was quite a philosophizer, the sailor was.

Fitzgerald once said to Hemingway, "Rich people are different from you and I." You and me, I think. Hemingway replied, "Yes, they have more money."

Writers are different from other people. They write. A writer's on set as a writer and not as a character. The narrator or main character is, in fact, another character in the book, but usually the most difficult to see because he is mistaken for the writer himself. The narrator is the writer's on-the-spot observer and often very uneasy in this role, at a loss to account for his presence.

Kerouac says in *Vanity of Duluoz*, "I am not I am, but just a spy in somebody's body pretending these sandbox games, kids in the cow field near St. Peter's church." He's just going through the motions of being a boy. He isn't a boy at all! So, he is watching the others pose for the camera. He will write them later.

When I first met Kerouac, he was twenty-one years old and had already written a million words. He was completely dedicated to his trade. He told me that I would write and call the book *Naked Lunch*. I did not think of myself as a writer, and told him so on many occasions.

I had tried writing a few pages now and then. Reading it over always gave me a sensation of aversion and disgust, such as a laboratory rat must feel when he chooses the wrong path and receives a sharp reprimand in his displeasure centers.

"I don't want to hear anything literary."

Kerouac just smiled and repeated that I'd write a book called *Naked Lunch*.

Thinking about that, you know, the 1940s seem centuries

away, so that I may be remembering a piece here and a piece five years later in another country: the bar on 116th Street, black wood tables in the booths, rum and Coca-Cola. Or was it in New Orleans?

Later, in Mexico, by the lake in Chepultepec Park, there is an island there where thousands of vultures roost apathetically. I was shocked at this sight since I'd always admired their aerial teamwork. Some skimming a few feet off the ground, others weaving way up, little black specks in the sky, and when they spot it, they pour down in a black funnel.

We are sitting at the edge of the lake with tacos and beer. I pointed at the vultures.

"They've given up like old men in St. Petersburg, Florida. Go out and hustle some carrion, you lazy buzzards!"

Whipping out my pearl-handled .45, I kill six of them in showers of black feathers. The other vultures took to the sky.

I would act these acts out with Jack, and quite a few of the scenes. What later appeared in *Naked Lunch* arose from these acts.

I remember we were in the University Club, of which I was a member, and a spastic member on a crutch got in the elevator, and I got the idea of tripping him and taking his crutch away and mimicking his twitches.

When Jack came to Tangiers in 1956, I decided to take his title and much of the book was already written.

I've been speaking of the role Jack Kerouac played in my script. The role I played in his can be inferred from the enigmatically pompous, Hubbardly betrayals which readily adapt themselves to the scenes between Carl and Dr. Benway in *Naked Lunch*.

Dr. Benway himself resulted from a much earlier collaboration with Kels Elvins, a high school and college friend — he always told me I should write. I used this almost verbatim in *Nova Express*: "You all all right?" he shouted, seeing himself among the women. "I'm a doctor."

Kerouac may have felt I did not include him directly in my cast of characters. However, there is much of Kerouac in William Lee.

"And we will all die and the stars will go out one after the other." I listened to Jack's prophesy like the winds can, rustling in the last white shadow.

Well, I've often been asked if I have some words of advice to young people, and I indeed have a few, young people and people of any age:

> Never interfere in a boy and girl fight.
> Beware of whores who say they don't want money.
> The hell they don't! What they mean is,
> they want more money. Much more.
>
> If you are doing business with a religious son-of-a-bitch,
> get it in writing. His word isn't worth a shit, not with the
> good Lord telling him how to fuck you on the deal.
>
> If, after being exposed to someone's presence, you feel as if
> you lost a quart of plasma, avoid that presence. You need
> it like you need pernicious anemia. I don't like to hear the
> word vampire around here. . . .

we (wē), *pron. pl.; possessive* **our** or **ours,** *objective* **us. 1.** nominative pl. of **I. 2.** (used by a speaker or writer to denote himself and another person or persons): *We have two children. In this block we all own our own houses.* **3.** (used to denote people in general): *the marvels of science which we t██ for gran██* **4.** (use█ to ████████ ██ particular profe█████, nation██ ██ politic█ █arty██, which includes the sp█████ or w███ *We in █e me█* *profession have moral ██nsi███i██.* **5.** █so cal█ ██████al **"we."** (used b█ ██v████ign██ ██y █her hig█ █ic█als and dignitaries, i███ █e ██ the '██ f█mal spe██ █ *We do not wear this crow█ ███out hu██* **6.** Als█ ████ed **the editorial "we."** (u███ █y editors ██ other wri██ ██ ██circumlocution for t█ █epetitive a█ too person█ ██. As for this column, we will have nothing to do with shady politicians.* **7.** you (used familiarly, often with the implication of mild █nd███ ██ ██ ████ ██ ██ ██ ██████ ██ ████ patient, a poseur, etc.): *We kn█w that's n██ghty, don't we? It's time we took our medicine. Aren't we testy?* **8.** (used in the predicate following a copulative verb): *It is we who should thank you.* **9.** (used in apposition with a noun, esp. for emphasis): *We humans are a sturdy species.* [ME, OE; c. D wij. G wir, Icel vēr, Goth weis]

ROBERT ANBIAN

WE

A Work-in-Progress

We

We thrive on flame,
glass and vapor biting
the hollows of our cheeks —
we're draping our skeletons
over the barrels of the firing squad,
nosotros, indio.
"When the dead are burned,
they writhe as if
trying to sit up."
The solitude of humanity
is making us armed
and beautiful.
We bulge with defeat.
We are the vein, the root,
the ax made of blood —
the word
against the Word —
the voice inside
the sex, the death,
the revolution
of us —
We are the negation
and the life —
the interruption

and the interrupting —
the never
and the tomorrow,
the yes, maybe,
the why not —

We

Betrayal our element,
we are the true of heart —
What ends continues,
what begins interrupts —
Everything spilling
into the abyss of the future.

A massacre already has occurred,
or will soon occur —
The postwar blues you are feeling
are perfectly normal —
Nous sommes tous sauvages.

We

Bronze disc
on a field of Red.

We

What?
The quality of memory
is not merciful. What? What?
We went walking in the neighborhoods
where the lawns are soft with blood.
What?
One world, one peace.
What? What?
The state of desire
is not represented on the flag.
What?
What?
(Pause: wait, wait,
wait, wait, wait,
wait, okay, now
quickly):
What?

We

Life, though mean,
is good.
Everyone wants the sky
to ripen with fruit
to blot out the heavens!
The corpses of the cousins 50 times removed
are sprouting branches

The rhythmic thumping of the women's pestles —
this was home.

We

Don't play away the sun
before the sunrise.
Don't eat the chicken
before it's hatched.
Don't discover a new world
before setting sail.
Don't set sail
before sinking the boat.
Don't get caught
between the fork and the meal.

We

Reach inside the jacket,
reach inside the vest,
something is there.
Reach inside the shirt,
reach inside the nipple,
reach inside the shoulder,
something's there.
Reach inside the arm,
reach inside the biceps,
reach inside the boney girdle —
something is there!
Reach inside the tissue,
reach inside the cartilage,
reach inside the splash of blood.
Something is there.
Reach inside the marrow,
reach inside the cell —
reach further! —
inside the shadow,
the charge, the emanation,
the transparent instant when
something is there.
Reach all the way through —

We

In the mind
there is always a moon
rolling over an horizon,
and one dusty yard
with two goats,
one black & white,
the other
white & black.

We

Soul full of seawater.
We went sailing round the world,
and the moon went flying
wherever we sailed.
We never lost sight
of the tear in our eye.

We

When you come to Tunis
we'll smoke some kif
*   — Apollinaire*

In Africa, we'll stroll the *marchés* by day,
the clubs *en plein air* by night
We'll go off with prostitutes,
one or two each,
we'll tremble
to touch their purple nipples
At dawn we'll let them
haggle us higher and higher
because we don't want them
to leave
We'll retreat to the dunes

by old fort Zinderneuf,
where the ex-presidents
are fainting over their meals
We'll go to the *quartier ancien*
and listen to the kora
and the hodu and the old griot
wailing tales of medieval wars

We'll go into the streets
and pay the player of the algaita
and the dundun drummers
and the singer of songs
to carry our praises
throughout the town
and up to the heavens
From the marabout
we'll seek out gris-gris
to protect us from knives,
scorpions, jealousy, the news
coming over the shortwave
We'll resolve never to want to go back
After dark we'll go down
to Madame Gilpain's
to argue about sex and colonialism
over bad red wine —
never forgetting *la fille* Gilpain —
until long after even
the drunken soldiers
have gone off to bed
We'll walk out into the night
where the desert is glowing
like a blue moon —

We

Everything unfolds
in the instant,
that scaramouche face
at the end of a bomb run
That flower of dust
above our scalps
O crosshairs
O crossroads
We sat together in the shelter
until long after
the lights had gone out,
our bodies touching
in the close air
We fell in love,
mingling our tongues
in way we could not have done
before the War
In the dark somewhere
someone crying,
just kept on weeping,
not loudly or in panic,
but persistently, quietly,
through all the stages
of the night

We

"The wind is blowing the hair
off my head, mother"
The gripe of avarice
has broken my back
We are passing away, mother!

We

White fish
in the North

We

Quiet . . . we must listen
for the slipping of the metals parts.
"Quiet, quiet, my love,
can't you see all the stars
are out tonight?
Wasn't I the one who taught you
to shoot the machine gun?"

We

Caminando, caminando . . .
> — *Victor Jara*

We, the panic
The struck-with-genius
The streaming-from-the-orange-dawn
The furious din
in the torn grass
The way the light fell
on the trampled ground
where already
we had passed
by
Walking, walking . . .
Buscamos libertad
Old us, this world
Mud full of heat
How long have we been arriving?
Caminando, caminando . . .
Go walking with death

and the heat
along the track
where the truck has broken down,
village choking in dust
Sun blazing
behind a pane of black glass
We had nothing
but limes
to suck on
Walking, walking . . .
Fabulous hat, peripatetic grave . . .
At night, we danced
in the road with the local yé-yé's
to a boombox highlife pulse
under the stars
By the kerosene glow,
all the villagers
jabbering, and the driver
and his one crewman
working, working
on the broken engine . . .

Walking, walking . . .
The poems of today
singing in our heads . . .

Drawing by Lawrence Ferlinghetti

THIS IS MY LAST POEM

J.T. GILLETT

1

Writing poetry is like a disease with no cure.
You let it run its course
and one day the fever breaks.
I've had the fever for twenty years.
I wrote hordes of wild, passionate poems.
I wrote square poems for square editors.
Radical poems for the revolution that does not exist.
Poems that begged for wine and music.

This is my last poem.
No American has written a decent poem
in twenty years and I'm tired of trying.
Poetry readings are boring. Real boring.
I've read flocks of my poems at poetry readings.
Jazzy poems. Shocking, surreal poems. Boring poems.
The New Yorker prints shitty poems.
Poetry journals are filled with shitty poems.
I've written lots of shitty poems
and this is my last one.
My magnum crappus. Grand finale. Final exit.
Exodus el poetus. Exile from poetic bondage.
Ode to the ultimate farewell.
My last poetic words. My last words on poetry.
My omega of poetry. My dirge of poetry.
My eschatology of poetry. My poetic coffin.
My shovel of dirt on poetry's grave.

This is my last poem and I feel better already.
Poetry sucks.

Most poets are O.K.
until they take themselves too seriously.
Then they turn into thirsty insects.
Poetry sucks poets dry. Really dry.
Does anyone have a glass of water? Cold beer?
Leave the bottle, because this is my last poem.
I'm tired of chasing verbs
through fields of bloodthirsty images.
No more swimming in swamps of syllabic scum.
No thanks.
This is my last encounter of the poetic kind.
I'm sick of hunting for metaphors
in the oozing stench
of bottom-feeding human perversions.
Poetry loves perversion and vice-versa.
Poetry is perversion and this is my last one.

The final arrow in my poetic quiver.
My swan poem. My poetic nightfall.
Finito del poeto. Endsville.
Total poetic zeroland.

I'm tired of getting high and trying to have visions.
I'm really tired of trying to remember visions
and write them down.
I'm not going to write them down any more.
I'm as serious as cancer: this is my last poem.

Poetry has no value in America.
Everyone in America writes a poem in the fourth grade
and gets a license to practice poetry
and knows just how valuable poetry really is
in the fourth grade they know
they really know everyone is a poet in America.

In Russia poetry readings
are performed in soccer stadiums.
100,000 comrades moved all at once
by a few good poets.
That's real value. Who needs the Marines.
I would consider moving to Russia
but this is my last poem and I will remain in America
where life is easy
where tattooed teenage rock stars with fake names
get paid millions of dollars to masturbate and scream
songs they don't even write
songs written twenty years ago, before they were born
while magnificent, visionary poets
go homeless and hungry and in jail.

Even the president is a poet in America.
Every judge is a poet in America.
Every cop is a poet in America.
Every dog is a poet in America.
Imagine this: everyone in America plays pro football
We have marvelous stadiums
in which to hold poetry readings
while pro football players
go homeless and hungry and in jail.

Imagine this: everyone in America has an eyeball
next to his asshole so he can clearly see
all the shit he puts out
so he can clearly see his poetic output.
This is my last poem and I'm sorry
but I have to say these things.

Even this, my bottom poetic dollar
has no value in America.
This 12-gauge shotgun to my poetic head.
This 12-inch curved dagger
to the fair-skinned throat of poetry.
A lethal injection of viral torture.
A shy kiss from a blue ring octopus.

A gentle push over a jagged cliff.
A terminal dose of instant karma.
This has got to be my last poem.

Once I believed my poems proved my existence.
Once I believed my poems were immortal.
But all my poems combined have no value in America.
No value in the free world.
No value unless accompanied by sex or money.
Yet this is it.
The Great White Light growing closer in the distance.
The poetic glow fading away
as if from the eyes of a dying monkey.

Once I believed my poems made a difference.
I believed that writing poems
made the world a better place for everybody.
Now I believe there are too many poems in America.
There's women's poetry
and gay poetry and black poetry.
There's Afro-american lesbian Christian poetry.
Hispanic poetry, Croatian poetry.
The poetry of Viet Nam vets.
The poetry of Vietnamese refugees
of Nicaraguan refugees
of psychedelic refugees
the surreal poetry of the American dream
the homeless poetry of a two-bedroom dumpster
the bankrupt poetry of global economies
the nuclear poetry of propulsion and trajectories
the melting fission poem of ground zero
the inevitable poem of lost continents
the poem that is spoken only at death
the only poem that counts.

2

Why did I start writing poems?
Why does anyone write poetry?
I believe poems choose someone to write them.
I believe poems choose someone to give them form
just like this poem chose me
to give it a place on this paper
to give it a voice in this room.

I believe that in the beginning there really was the Word
and when the Word sought beauty
the first poem was created
and it was a perfect poem
that reached deep into your soul
every phrase so clear and sublime
that just one line made you weep
reading the whole poem could blind the strongest men
or rejuvenate the weak of heart.
It was a powerful poem that created
every amoebic alliteration
every allegorical allegation
every juvenile juxtaposition
every synaptic simile
every monad of hyperbole
every molecular rhyme
every gang of cells
making goo-goo eyes in the plasmic night.
The perfect poem moved entire hemispheres
shifted the earth's axis
altered the orbits of galaxies
and inspired the first true love and madness.

Every poem that has called man to action
every poem that has stirred a generation
incited a riot and started a revolution
every poem that has actually reached out
and changed the course of history

every great poem is part of the perfect poem
every Song of Myself and Season in Hell
every Howl and Coney Island of the Mind
all of William Blake's poems
are born of that first perfect poem.
And all poets, whether they know it or not
search for the perfect poem
and want to caress it and hold it down
and call it their own.
I have stalked the perfect poem many times.
Yes, I saw it once.
It came to me like a seizure
and just a few words made me dizzy.
It is the Holy Grail of poems
the Emerald Tablets of poems
the Great Pyramid of poems
the Philosopher's Stone of poems
the ancient cabala of poems
the Skull and Roses of poems
its truth and necessity crushed me
like the weight of the solar system.
I reached for a pen and paper.
I wanted to cage the magic words
but they escaped me like smoke
from an open window.
I never saw them again.
I hunt the almighty poem no more.
My quest for the great mover has expired.
But I do believe the perfect poem will be found
or maybe another piece of it will appear
and we'll know it when we hear it.
Yes, everyone in America will know the perfect poem
as if it was a rock star.

I hope nobody is waiting for my next poem
because it does not exist.
But all my poems are better than this one.
Take my word for it.

This is my last poem and that's all that matters.
Does it matter if the kamikaze
performs an exquisite final descent?
Does it matter if the paisley parachute almost opens?
The spitting cobra misses your eyes before it strikes?
Does it matter if a legal overdose is unintended?
Imagine this: a friendly missile
traveling at the speed of light
lands right on top of your head.
You never heard it coming.
You never saw the flash.
Does it matter if a mushroom cloud is not symmetrical?

Some things just run their course.
Close up shop. Cease and desist. Hang up the fiddle.
I grab the ragged curtain of poetry with my teeth
and pull it through the floor.

I burst the elite bubble of poetry with my dick
and set the whole played out mess to rest
a soft, satiny pillow smothering poetry's sweet face.
It's easier than you think to write your last poem.
It's not like writing Revelations
or the knock-out poem of eternal blackness
and unconditional love.
It's not like being part of anything cool
like the Beat Generation.
Nothing at all like that.

And it's definitely not like jumping headfirst
off the top of the Mark Anthony Hotel
or drinking two quarts of whiskey a day
at your mom's house.
It's just my last poem.
The butt, the tail, the crack of doom
fait accompli, hasta la vista, baby, adios.

A simple sayonara of pennies shining on my poetry's eyes.
A little something for the ferryman: keep the change.

When Robert Frost was twenty years old
he proclaimed he would become a real poet
by the time he was thirty
or he would find another profession.
I heard that story when I was seventeen
and it sounded very noble.
I am thirty-seven years old now
and it sounds like public relations.
Either way, the poetic journey is more sweet than cruel.
And because I believe poetry is a good investment
In one's soul
and because this is the sunset of my forevering
and because I have no choice
I will always see poetry
in the wrinkles of my bed sheets.
I will seek unspeakable adventures
I may even chance upon the perfect poem
but I will never write another poem.

I take a very deep breath
and consider the death of a close friend.
The incredible loss and suffering we must endure.
The fear and loathing.
I am lucky I am only losing my last poem.

I take a very deep breath and remember Allen Ginsberg.
"Listen to the silence between your breaths,"
he said, "that is the source of pure poetry."
I sit very still and listen to the silence
between my breaths. I listen for a long time
and hear only silence
as if nothing really does add up to nothing
and that's really all there is.
It is time to rest a while and shut up.
I close my eyes, cut the cord

and watch my last poem take its final, quiet breath
as all the poems I've ever written flash before my eyes.

3

Cutting the cord that feeds your last poem
is like slashing your wrists.
If you cut in the wrong direction
if you miss the artery
if you misjudge the geometry of death
you will not ring the silver bell.
You will not send your victim to sleep with the angels.
You will not let her go.

Poetry is like a woman who won't go away
like a woman who sends me to the moon.
Poetry is like a woman who is horribly good
like a dark, spooky woman
a soft-spoken, strong woman
a vivacious, voluptuous woman
who knows the ultimate secret
a vicious vampire woman
who is on close personal terms with pain
a woman who knows how to dance the lambada
a woman who knows how to fake it
a woman who doesn't know what she wants
a woman who knows how to get it anyway.

Poetry is like a woman who wants to see me bleed.
A heroic woman, a generic woman
an exotic woman, an erotic woman.
She is every poet's sweetheart
she is every poet's whore.
She opens her arms, spreads her legs
and wiggles her toes.
She double flips off the high-wire
and lands in a bed of soft wet kisses.

Locker room incense burns the air.
The deep pulse of heavy breathing
rises from her soul: the soul of poetry.

I cannot kill this poem.
I cannot harm the gentle bird that wakes me.
I cannot will this poem to die.
I cannot click my heels and make it go away.
This poem is like the Elvis who keeps showing up.
I can only abandon this poem
like my first car
like immortal childhood friends.
I can only abandon this poem like old skin.

I buy my last poem a one-way ticket to Graceland.
I take it to the bus station.
I watch it fade away into the blue sequin sunset.
I imagine my last poem
kicking and screaming in the back seat
its sad face pressed to the window.
Maybe I should have sent it to Las Vegas.
I watch to make sure it doesn't come back
and feel my last poem in the silence all around me.

No blame. No regrets.
Gratitude and happiness in every direction.

4

Losing my last poem is more like losing a finger
than like losing an appendix.
Losing my last poem makes me queasy.
The nausea of happiness
is the first symptom of creative madness.
Disaster is an energy source.
Hallucinations bloom under stress.

Painters knew this and to prove it they cut off their ears
and every painter started their own school of painting.
Painting has been fifty years ahead of poetry ever since.
I started my own school of poetry
and tried to catch up with all those painters
and I found out the photographers
had already shot the cans out from under the painters.
I am the only student in my school of poetry.

Painters and photographers are welcome to attend.
My school of poetry will close forever
when I abandon this poem once and for all.

Who is this "I" that writes this poem?
Whose voice do I really hear
when I close my eyes and listen?
When I close my eyes and try to find
the next lines of this poem
when I try to find the perfect ending for this poem
when I try to find the words
that say everything that must be said
the beautiful words that will make you shiver.

Where does this poetic voice come from?
Oral hallucinations come from the right side of the brain
but how do they get there?
I do not know.

Imagine this: the poetic voice inside my head is a recording.
All the poems I ever wrote were pre-recorded
and I just listen to them inside my head
and believe they belong to me.

Maybe this poem will not end with a bang.
Maybe it will end with a

hiss.

Imagine this: the poetic voice inside my head
is the voice of God
spoken long ago and received by my brain
like my brain is a cheap radio
and God is a heavenly DJ
and His show ricochets around the universe
and lands inside somebody's head purely by chance.
Maybe the poetic voice inside my head is recorded by God.
Maybe poets only transcribe God's message machine.
Maybe the poetic voice inside my head
is not recorded by God.
Maybe it is recorded by regular angels.
Maybe bad guys hijack the poetic airwaves regularly.

Imagine this: insects are really the best poets.
Their antennas tune in to primo airwaves.
Cockroach poetry must be really intense.
Imagine the frantic poems of their colonies.
The magnificent love poems ants write for their queen
the rich, sweet poetry of the hive
the humble, melancholy poem of the praying mantis
the unquenchable, high-voltage poem of the cicada
graceful midnight poems of fireflies
annoying litile mosquito poems
gorgeous poems of corpse-eating blowflies.

My last poem is like a centipede
crossing a busy street
and every car just misses it by a breath
until finally it gets to the other side
and a boy on a bicycle squishes its rear end
and it is just able to drag itself to a safe haven
when a hubcap flies off the last Yugo in America
and lands right over my centipede
like a rusty mausoleum
like a roadside memorial
like a requiem for what might have been
like a rhapsody for the next world.

5

My name is J.T. Gillett
and I just want to know why I'm really here.
My name is J.T. Gillett
and there are lots of people out there
telling me I'm here for different reasons.
They tell me I'm somebody I don't always know.
They tell me I'm somebody I don't always like
but sometimes I don't know or like my own poems.
My name is J.T. Gillett
and I just want to know why I am writing this poem
when invisible viruses
have declared war on my species
when slate-wiping viruses
are spreading in the jungle
when entire tribes are wiped out by viruses
that make you bleed to death through your eyes
when these viruses are one day away via air express
when millions of viruses fit on the head of a pin
like Manhattan at rush hour
everybody shopping for a gracious host.

Bill Burroughs says language is a virus from outer space.
I just want to know why I am writing about viruses
when I could be watching reruns of Gilligan's Island
or reading Mondo 2000.
I just want to know why I am writing my last poem
when there is so much beginning to do.
So many do do birds swallowed by extinction.
Every day so many absolute fade-aways
creation is precious, every moment so complete
endless moments in every minute
all dying
all sentient beings
all dying
all things (including those that don't exist)
all dying

Ashland dying
Oregon dying
San Francisco dying
redwoods dying
Pacific Ocean dying
good clean air dying
ozone dying
Grateful Dead dying
I'm dying
you're dying
this poem is slowly dying
rock 'n roll says it's not dying
but I'd double-check the pulse.
There are so many ways to prove I am alive
so many ways to use my body
these hands, ears, tongue and eyes
there are so many ways
to feel the music
and fall from the window
there are so many ways
for my last poem to hit the ground.
I can almost hear its final word
a whisper reflected upward
from an empty sidewalk.
I can almost hear its final echo
just after it hits the concrete.

6

How should I spend my last poem?
Should I aim my last poem at some heavenly bulls-eye?
Should I try to save a rain forest?
Or is my last poem an aimless assassin
stalking a nonexistent enemy
my drive-by shooting poem
taking lazy potshots at random targets.
My armed and dangerous kamikaze poem
my kamikaze poem that never misses.

My kamikaze poem cannot go down alone.
My kamikaze poem wants to settle some scores.
My kamikaze poem knows this is its last blast
and it wants its money's worth
it wants somebody big to get what's coming
it wants to lay the smoking guns on the broken table
it wants to put some ex-presidents in jail
it wants Nixon to pay for the Kent State massacre
it wants Reagan to dig up some mass graves
in the jungles of El Salvador
it wants George Bush to share a cell with Manuel Noriega
it wants Dan Quayle to share a cell with Charles Manson
it wants to dig up J. Edgar Hoover live on CNN
while famous newspeople
read an endless list of police atrocities.

We are harassed by cops
every time we see one in the rear view mirror
every time we park our car on a city street
every time they hide behind bushes with radar guns
we are harassed by cops.
We are harassed by a defense industry
that wants to kill us all.
Harassed by a CIA that wants to put bombs in space.
Harassed by an IRS that wants to take our money
to create more devices to kill us from greater distances.
By a government that knows what's best for you and me.
By a government that wants us to buy more TVs
so we can watch it all go down from a safe distance.
Baghdad bombed after dark so we can see the fireworks
but we can't see the maimed babies
we can't see the innocent bodies piled high in the streets.
We are harassed by a government
that wants us to buy more cigarettes
and more booze and more guns.

Government keeps the ghetto full of crack and smack
throws us in jail for smoking pot
Jails are full of pot smokers and victimless criminals
these are political prisoners, these are political prisoners
there are more political prisoners in America
than in any other country in the world.

There are more people in American jails
than in Russian jails
There are more people per capita in jail in America
than in any other country in the world.
They are building more jails all the time.
Prisons are already a commercial enterprise in America.
There are more cases of mistaken identity
than ever before.
You could be next. Your sons and daughters. Or mine.

This is my last poem and I want to spend it on freedom.
Not freedom in the theoretical or absolute sense.
Not any Platonic ideal or categorical imperative.
Not even constitutional freedom (ha ha ha).
I would like to spend my last poem
doing exactly what I am doing.
That's the freedom I want to buy with my last poem.
The freedom I can feel in every pore of my body.
It's not much.
Just buying a little time.
A temporary state of grace.
My last poetic wad blown without reservation
blazed with total disregard for rules and regulations
total disregard for friendly suggestions
total disregard for the possibility of publication
my last poem dancing with total abandon until it drops.

7

My last poem may be the humble beginning
of a manic explosion of last poems
all diving headfirst into oblivion
a slithering orgy of last poems
thrusting themselves out of this world
waking up out of their bodies.
Yes, yes, I invite all poets to join me
and let your last poems bloom.
Let there be last poems about sitting on the couch
eating tofu hot dogs
watching intelligent cheerleader movies
betting on metaphysical football games
running for mayor of unknown cities
and plotting sweet revolutions.
Imagine this: vast gardens of last poems
veining around skyscrapers
like whirling Babels of last poems
colossal brambles of last poems
taking over the White House.
Armies of young Republicans
cutting down forests of last poems
but the last poems strip them naked
and slap their white asses.
They try to poison their roots
but they just slap harder
and grow back stronger.
Glorious hallelujahs of last poems.
Platoons of last poems
marching in tight formation.
Wild bands of last poems
running crazy in every direction.
Last poems taking over TV stations.
Last poem trading cards available everywhere.
Multi-national alliances of last poems.
Coalitions of last poem cartels.
Interstellar conspiracies of last poems.
Last poems coming back from the dead.

Yes, yes, I invite all poets to join me
and write their last poems!
Even if you've never written a poem before!
(don't hesitate, start right now!)
It's never too late to write your last poem.
May all poems be last poems
may last poems gush forth
may last poems never end
may streets overflow with last poems!
Last poems will bury police cars.
Last poems will eat the rich and rewrite history.
Last poems will make the world a better place.
They will accurately forecast
the consequence of here and now.
They will always tell the truth.
They will bring heaven to earth
Just like in the old days
when we believed the world
was going to end very soon
and poetry would live forever.

[To be continued]

NORMAN NAWROCKI

THE BLACK FLAGG

Hello.
Are you bothered by sleepless nights,
Yuppies gnawing away at your neighborhood?
Do you suffer from nightmares about being
roasted alive at a Yuppie barbecue?
Do you go bananas when you hear Yuppies gnashing
their BMW gearboxes or popping champagne corks
to toast new condos on your block?
If so, then you've got a problem
and you need a proven Yuppie pest control:

THE BLACK FLAGG

Comes with a heavy-duty, no-nonsense stainless steel
flag pole good for 100 Yuppie exterminations.

THE BLACK FLAGG

when used properly,
will unleash unruly punk rockers, riff raff,
condo evictims, old-age pensioners and
general malcontents and provoke immediate panic
in any nest of Yuppies.
Plant it on a Yuppie lawn, and you can raise hell
'til the break of dawn.
Plant it through their tinted windshields
and watch their smiles crumble.
Plant it through the tips of their Gucci shoes
and hear them holler. (Ha ha)
Plant it through the front door of their condos
and watch them scurry away and hide in the bathroom.

THE BLACK FLAGG

The people's choice. Used for centuries by
leading professionals everywhere, from the
Paris Commune to the streets of Chicago and LA.
Works where other pest controls fail.
It's odorless, too, and will not destroy the ozone.

DON'T LET A DIM-WITTED YUPPIE MAKE YOUR
    LIFE MISERABLE.
Fight back.
Use THE BLACK FLAGG, and shove it up their
brand name Yuppie ass.
Comes with a smart, two-tone vinyl carrying case.
Don't be the last on your block to fly one.

THE BLACK FLAGG

Get yours today.

ALBERTO BLANCO

5 POEMS

Music in the Age of Iron

To Gabriel Macotela

This isn't the wind in the willows
nor that of the eucalyptus
nor even the wind that brightens sails
and moves the slow windmills.

Nor is it the wind that propels clouds
in summer's calendar
nor the dawn's wind
rising with the birds.

Brothers, sisters
this is not the song of autumn
nor the sighing of lovers
who embrace in moonlight.

This isn't the song of snowflakes
nor the alternating dance of day and night,
nor the slow rhythm of your breath
and my breath . . . listen:

It is the voice of cities sick to death
— of steel sheets, rods and blocks —
the inevitable motor and the discord
of an epoch in disarray.

It is the trite humming that finds
an echo of change in the Apocalypse:
the Kingdom of Speed
and the opposed signs of time.

It is the insensate noise of industry
— the factories exploited past reckoning —
traces of rot and insidious gases,
the factories, not you or I.

Uproar, friction and mist amid the machinery
— hideous shriek of this empty age —
in this bottomless barrel. It is
the international tongue of usury.

The new universal tongue:
esperanto of infamy
— wires, axes, chains —
the age of iron knows no other voice.

But the descent can't go on forever
because even noise has its limits . . . listen:
this isn't the wind in the willows
nor that of the eucalyptus . . .

Nothing Happens

To Carla Rippey

Life is a film in black and white
where you can't read the subtitles
so it seems that death doesn't rest
in light or in darkness.

Small worlds start spinning
on the edge of dream
with the wind of grief
and a rush toward memory.

But nothing happens . . .
There in the depth of the screen
there is no possible accusation
nor a couple's mortal sadness.

Just a thirst for images
softly diminishing
in the fountains of custom
where words take on flesh.

Lilith

To Liliana Mercenario

Like a mirror waiting
for the earth to fall asleep
to return it, cleansed, to the waters
of the sea that reaches between brow and brow

I take refuge in your eyes:
quietly, slowly, I approach
the hollow where a wounded deer weeps,
lost in the forest of your hair . . .

And although I cannot touch your soul
I know the forms of your dreams
on that lonely, fantastic beach
where night and dawn make silent love.

Nostalgia

To Arturo Rivera

There is the sky. Now I can see it.

There is the open sky
waiting for the best I can give.

Left behind are parents,
friends, givers of advice.

The dreamt toys of childhood,
the tree of desire,
night in the depths of the pool,
the park that witnessed our first kiss . . .

I see it all in the distance
like a body that awakens
in a remote part of a landscape.
I look at it as if it were false.

We have arrived at life
by saying farewell to all we have loved,
to that which was given,
to all those we love.

But there, at this moment, the sky.

Immersed Flame

A reflector searching the darkness
    of an ordinary day
or a luminous stain on the silver
    of a forgotten mirror
    in a darkened alcove

Such is the flame of silence

A lighted match in one's hands
    on a evening stroll
or a gust of fresh air
    among the swollen clouds
    of a dim suburban landscape

Such is the flame of silence

Like those fish
    that in the sea's bottom
        are their own light

Translated by Julian Palley

ED SANDERS

CHEKHOV

1

The Phantom from Taganrog

Who was this man
        called Chekhov
                in the time-mist

Who was this very energetic guy
from a little grain-port
            on the Sea of Azov?

We glimpse him
        in his stories and plays,
        in the 4,000 letters that survived

        and in the words of Gorky,
        Bunin, Suvorin, his sister Maria,
        his brothers Michael and Alexander
                and a few hundred others

The life of a genius
can swerve for 10,000 pages
& yet you're looking at sand

It's not clear what he was
except a writer and survivor
        who lived his productive years
                to the constant throb
        of the TB doom-drum

who told his tales
            wrote his plays
            built schools and clinics
                  tended the rubleless sick

His life as complicated
            as any genius
                  with a racing metabolism
and the ever quick'ning throb
                  of the TB drums

      This phantom from Taganrog
      whom we call out to
            100 years down
                  into the mist

54

1900

Chekhov and Tolstoy were elected
            honorary members
                  of the literary section
of the Academy of Sciences
                  early in the year.

Pining for Olga
Chekhov proposed that the Art Theater
tour the sticks, including the Crimea.
Stanislavsky finally agreed and
            Olga and Anton were together in early April.

*

Olga Came to Yalta in July of '00

They met in Yalta again in July, till August 5.

      Each night they met

                              in his study
          she in her long white dress
                    that showed off her curly erotic hair
          She'd humm-sing Glinka's "Don't Tempt Me In Vain,"

They fucked
and whispered softly with
                         hands entwined

They'd try to stay discrete
                    in the quiet house
with laughter & kisses & shussshes
               coffee and bread at midnight
               and then up the creaking staircase
                              to their separate rooms

                              *

          The Fascination Continued

          Olga danced
          herself
                    short of breath
          in a plunging neckline
                         the fall of '00

          and wrote about it
                    breathlessly to her
                              short-of-breath
                                   playwright beau

                              *

October 16,
          he finished the final dialogue
                    for *The Three Sisters*
and hastened to Moscow
for a six-week stay at the Hotel Dresden

There was a reading of
                    the play
in the Art Theater's lobby

and then after it was over
there was a nervous silence
the coughs of actors
                    and toe-stare

Some were not sure whether
it was a tragedy or a comedy

"It's not really a play yet,
                    it's more of an outline,"
                                    someone said.

Chekhov sulked away
but rewrote much of the first
                                    two acts

                    *

The early-hitting Moscow winter
drove him to Nice on the Riviera
in December

It was partly the lure of fleeing
that drove him,
            & partly the pressure of
                        Three Sisters final revisions
and partly the lung-soothing clime.

From Nice to Florence and Rome
and then back to Yalta
                    "to write and write."

                    *

On Dec. 24, 1900
Lenin and the Marxists
            began *Iskra (The Spark)*

It was printed with small, crowded type
                on onionskin
                        for easy smug/dist

and a secret network
            was set up
                    to get it to readers
throughout the Russian empire

55

Olga Knipper and Marriage

1901

January 31, the premiere of *The Three Sisters*
                    at Moscow Art Theater.

*

On March 4, Cossacks charged students
                in front of St. Petersburg's Kazan Cathedral
        lashing with their *nagaiki*
The students were protesting new laws
                    restricting academic freedom —

Gorky wrote Chekhov an eyewitness account:

        Cossacks grabbed women by the hair
                    and whacked them with whips
        They smashed into the protestors
                in front of Petersburg's Kazan Cathedral
                                    killed two

*

At the end of March Olga
    came for ten days to Yalta

She was eager to get married
    and avoid the ritual
        of the creaking staircase

*

    May 25, Olga and Anton were married
            in a church in Moscow.
    He did not tell his sister or mom
    Bride and groom took a train to the East
    to visit Maxim Gorky for a day
        (under house arrest for
          taking part in the March demonstrations)

    then down the Volga
        to a sanitorium
            for the "Koumiss cure."

*

Maria Chekhov viewed her brother's marriage
about as sourly
    as Dorothy Wordsworth

*

    Koumiss is fermented mare's milk
      borrowed from the people of the steppes
      who originally made it from camel's milk

    For a month he drank four bottles a day
        and stopped coughing almost entirely

    then they returned to Yalta.

Olga went to Moscow in the early fall for rehearsals
and a time-sparged modern marriage

She was already
            one of the most famous of her time.

Actresses in Russia
were treated to Total Adoration —
twenty minute curtain calls
Audiences that wept actual tears

She loved it
She could not give up the thrill

"I am not young enough
            to shatter
                  in one second
      what it has taken me such pains
                        to achieve."

                      *

"If you and I
      cannot live together,"
                  he wrote her
"it is neither you nor I
who are guilty
but the demon
            who fills me
with bacilli
      and you with the love of art."

                      *

            Their time-tracks met thereafter
            in supercharged sections
            rather than a long, ropy
                        taffypull

"To Moscow! To Moscow!"

He lived the winter of '03-'04 in Moscow
The writer Ivan Bunin spent just about
every night with Chekhov
> Olga would party
> and come home at 3 or 4 AM

"Every evening I visit Chekhov
and stay with him till three or four AM
Until Olga Leonardova came home

She usually went to the theater
or to a charity concert

Nemirovich-Danchenko would fetch her
in white tie and tails
smelling of cigars and eau-de-Cologne

She wore an evening dress,
> beautiful, young and scented

I would kiss her hand and they would leave
Chekhov would never let me go before
> > their return."

*

> To Ivan Bunin
> dry eyes, no tears:
> "I'll be forgotten in seven years."

*

One Reason for Cigarettes

In December of '03
a right wing nut tried to stab Gorky

as he walked along the Volga at night

The knife pierced his coat and jacket
                    but was blunted
                            by Maxim's cigarette case.

*

Party Time

There was a New Year's party at
                    The Moscow Art Theater
                            early in '04
They feasted
        then danced

The beautiful Olga was asked to the floor
while Chekhov and Gorky
tried to talk o'er the music and party purr
Soon both were coughing
                            coughing coughing
Chekhov leaned over to
    the author of *The Lower Depths*:

"People might say of us,
'They exchanged some highly interesting coughs.'"

*

Aeschylus — Part IV
The Cherry Orchard

Chekhov attended rehearsals,
            didn't like what they were doing to his play
& Stanislavsky didn't like Chekhov butting in.

There's a problem
when an author thinks he's written a comedy
and the director thinks it's a social drama

on the downfall of the getting-poor gentry class
while New Age money-hawks
hawk-seize the land and money.

*

Strokes, Folks

Stanislavsky had called it
"a truly great tragedy"

Chekhov had replied,
"It is a farce."

62

1904

The Cherry Orchard premiered January 17
                his 44th birthday.
                        at the Moscow Art Theater
Chekhov stayed home.
        At the end of Act 2 Stanislavsky and Nemirovich-Danchenko
                sent him a note that th' audience had been
                        calling for him

He arrived at the end of Act 3,
                was hurrahed onstage,
while the audience cheered and thunder-clapped,
the author striving mightily not to cough

There were gifts and flowers in piles in front of him,
and speeches of glorification from
        journalists, actors and heads of literary societies
in a contest of quick-planned praise
There was an element in it as if he were already
                                in the grave.

It took an hour, and Chekhov could not say a word,
                        but left the footlights exhausted.

                              *

The Russo-Japanese War of '04

Both countries thirsted
                to thrust into Manchuria and Korea
Japan attacked the Russian fleet
and made much death and ship-sink
                another humiliation for Russia

about which the failing Chekhov
                was very little attentive

"It is not the Russian people, but the Autocracy
that has suffered shameful defeat,"
                        Lenin wrote.
"This defeat is the prologue to the
                capitulation of Tsarism!!"

                              *

The Cherry Orchard was touring the provinces to full houses.

                He ever more greatly
                        had trouble breathing
                He'd quake with fever
                Acute pains in his arms and legs

                His doctor gave him morphine
                        shoot-ups

        yet the brain-vim
                could not be killed
        He wrote oodles of letters

        and arranged for more books to be sent

to the Taganrog library
and scanned and marked up manuscripts
                    for *Russkaya mysl.*
                    (*Russian Thought*)

*

Body Fading, Brain Boiling

Toward the end
he was glutted with visitors.

too weak to write
though he hatched new plays in his mind
and recopied in ink his notebooks

*

He told Bunin,
"I'm going away to peg out."

Bunin thought he went
        so as not to die in front of his family.

*

On June 3rd
        with Olga by train
                to a German health resort
                        at Badenweiler
                                in the Black Forest

June 29 a hideous body-wracking attack.
the doctor gave him morphine and O_2

then another wracking.

He told his bank in Berlin
        to make all payments in his wife's name.

*

At the same time
Vladimir Lenin
    and his wife Krupskaya
began a month-long walk.
with knapsacks, through the Swiss countryside

Lenin was near a nervous breakdown
              from months of shrilly-dilly factionalism

and allowed the waterfalls, the blue lakes,
the glaciers: Geneva to Lausanne to Interlaken
to Lucerne
          — in the whirling patterns of Gaia
             to ease the mania.

63

At 2 AM the doctor arrived.
Chekhov covered in sweat,
and spotting the doctor
Chekhov sat up,
leaned against his pillows,
and said, "Ich sterbe."

The doctor gave him a
           camphor injection
and was sending for an
           oxygen pillow

but Chekhov said,
"What's the use?
Before it arrives
      I'll be a corpse."

In response Dr. Schwohrer
sent for champagne,
Chekhov held a glass
and said to Olga
"It's been so long since
              I've had champagne,"

and ever slowly drank it down
then lay upon his side

A black-winged moth
had come through the window
and was beating
          its wild wings
                    against the lamp.

JEREMY REED

BOWIE BALLARD WARHOL
Film Takes

1

A black sky above a white earth. The introductory voice effects to Bowie's *Sound And Vision* anticipate a silver Lamborghini being driven in a dust-cloud across the landscape. Several aluminum pyramids show on the horizon. As the camera zooms in so the giant image of Warhol, hands placed over his cock, is cut across by lightning.

2

Bowie is seen leaning up against the base to a pyramid. He lights a cigarette in slow motion, his gelled hair falling in strands across his forehead. He appears to be waiting for something or someone. He watches a shooting star travel across space before breaking into song. He sings *The Speed Of Life* while the camera angles in on Ballard wearing dark glasses behind the wheel of the Lamborghini.

3

The passenger seat is empty, but the camera tracking finds the novelist looking behind him. Monroe is sitting in the rear-seat, her fishnet-stockinged legs arched up high with Bowie sitting next to her in a silver dress as the music changes to *Ashes To Ashes*.

4

When the scene changes, the car is seen burning on an area of wasteland. Warhol is filming the metallic pyre, while Ballard films Warhol and Bowie films Ballard. Arc intrudes into the picture. He carries a mannequin with a grotesquely erect penis and deposits it in the fire. Fighter jets crash over while Bowie breaks into *Heroes.*

5

The interior of a hotel suite. The room is full of masks and mannequins. Ballard is examining a blueprint. Warhol toys with a rotating square globe. Bowie sits in a corner, writing into a word processor. Someone stripped to the waist in tight jeans, stands painting with his back to the company. When he turns round his face is a tin can.

6

Warhol is viewed silkscreening in the desert. He is working on his wrecked car series, while Ballard looks on as a detached spectator. Dressed in a black leather jacket, black shades, a striped tie tucked into jeans, the artist is seen transforming images to a canvas painted with a single gloss of livid colour. *Vertical Orange Car Crash, Green Disaster Twice, Purple Jumping Man, Lavender Disaster* — the poetics of these lavender, pink, mint-green and orange paintings are obsessively magnified in clear, blurred or misaligned images Ballard stares fixedly at the burning cars repeated twenty times on a single canvas.

7

Warhol is viewed in bed with Mr. X. The man lies face down to the pillow so as to remain unidentified. A Chanel № 5 bottle is enlarged to the point of being the only object in the room.

8

Music blows across Ballard shopping at a late-night supermarket. It is Stacey Heydon's guitar intro to *Station To Station* which follows the writer from the delicatessen to the wines and spirits positioned before check-out. When he comes out into the High Street the figure of Arc as a pilot with his long hair tied back in a pony-tail follows Ballard across the traffic stalled by a green go-light. The pilot splits into a multiple succession of clones. The sky registers a ruby and turquoise detonative flash as a helicopter nosedives into a concrete television block. It breaks up into a suspended fall-out of burning debris.

Bowie clippage as the Ziggy androgyne in his farewell concert at the Hammersmith Odeon in 1973 is interspersed with the delirium of crowds storming the car in which his double is driven away. As the car accelerates through urban streets the face at the wheel is seen to be Ballard's.

Shots of Marilyn stripping in the Grand Hotel are replayed in a voyeuristic sequence. Her glass sheer stockings are run off her legs as silk cocoons. She stands facing the mirror in a deep black lace suspended belt and black panties. On her bottom two red lipstick *f*s are made to imitate Man Ray's photograph: *Ingres' Violin*.

Arc is seen narrowing his camera between Marilyn's legs. On the black counterpane to their bed are arranged the miniature German officers discovered as a collector's toys in a felt-lined case in a bedside drawer. Each wears a swastika on his uniform. The lens blows them up to life size. A swastika is positioned above Marilyn's shaved pubis. Beside her is a copy of the Bowie bootleg, *Nazi Heroically*.

Bowie's *Station To Station* slashes across Lou Reed's *White Light White Heat*. The visual accompaniment is that of a mannequin dressed as a clown in scarlet puffed sleeves and a pointed gold hat. In its left hand stands a model of Adolf Hitler, arm raised in salute.

The labyrinthine anfractuosities of the stone forest are explored. Coral steeples, spires resembling Giacometti sculptures, environmental art, Martian graffiti.

Ballard stands looking up into the glide-ways. A Jumbo is beginning its descent over the city. Edited into this are shots of Yves Saint Laurent in his white cotton over-jacket, concentratedly sketching at his board, surrounded by Walter Glod robots.

A coffin-shaped map of New York indicates in scarlet lettering the places that Andy Warhol frequented. They flash up with the delayed time spacing of information relays at an airport. Bloomingdale's — Lexington Avenue, Vito Giallo's Antique Shop — 966 Madison Avenue, Jewellery District — West 47th Street, Le Cirque — 58 East 65th Street, Trump Tower — 725 Fifth Avenue, F.A.O. Schwartz toy shop — 767 Fifth Avenue. Warhol is seen handing out copies of *Interview* to New York passers-by. A junkie in a red fur coat stops by, opens it to show that she is wearing nothing but stockings. When her lowered head is raised to camera level the face is seen to be Marilyn's.

The fragmentary narrative moves to the ruined villas along the coast. Gap-roofed, missing walls, figurative totems lodged amongst sunflowers in the gardens. The atmospherics build to the sound of Iggy Pop's *Some Weird Sin*, stills of Aleister Crowley seen with Hitler at the Abbey of Thelema, then a series of multiple images depicting the world leaders sitting waiting in a nuclear dug-out for the heat flash. They watch Arc's film, share out the sachets of powdered protein, exchange snapshots and discreetly masturbate. A robot programmed to administer euthanasia shots is screened off in an adjoining cubicle.

17

Another zoom shot of the stone desert. A black sun is mounted on the pointed apex of a reef. A photograph of Jean Cocteau is seen looking out from the centre. He is reading Ballard's *Myths of the Near Future*. His waist is joined to the celebrated picture of Monroe's white dress blowing up above her thighs.

18

A series of high-speed takes, dubbed over with audio facilities shows Arc's facial planes scrambled into fragmented images; his dark glasses acting as a light reflector. The facets jump into abbreviated visuals. He is blown away into molecular components. When he rematerializes, he is viewed with a solarized body, a turtle shell strapped to his back, his direction a slow crawl towards a disused railway station.

19

Crash. A reconstructed slow replay action of Jayne Mansfield's death. The collisional force of the two cars resembles a log jammed into an alligator's snout. On the billboard by the roadside are posters of James Dean and Albert Camus. A head without a body makes rabbit leaps across the ground and disappears.

20

A green sky over Monte Carlo. Helmut Newton is observed photographing a model on a terrace overlooking the bay. Dressed in black stockings and pivoting on stilettos, she smokes a cigar. The spectator on the opposite roof walks a leopard round the flat rectangle. Its collar and leash sparkle with rhinestones.

A girl with her legs arched over her head in a half-somersault runs a red fingernail across her black panties, while the other hand fits inside her stocking top. A mannequin is positioned watching the girl; an erect silver phallus strapped into place. The figure of Warhol standing behind the girl is making his own obsessive film centered on the silver dildo.

22

Trisexual accomplishments. A man is seen making love to a woman on a voluminous hotel bed. She is Indonesian. Her black hair falls straight to her waist. She is up on her haunches. He eases in and out of her and is seen drawing a scarlet loveheart in lipstick on her bottom. On the next bed a man in a platinum Warhol wig is blowing another whose cock is sheathed in a star-patterned condom. On the third bed two women engage in sensuous love. The submissive partner beneath is veiled by a black face-net. Her active partner is seen from behind, her tongue flicking over magenta areolas, her skin-tight leather skirt raised above her bottom. The photographic scene blacks out to images of Bowie, Ballard and Warhol staring from a wall in the dark.

JEREMY REED

BURROUGHS

Bullet holes pepper the shotgun painting —
a yellow shrine with a black continent
patched up on wood.
The suit's impeccable, no lazy tie,
the knot perfect between blue collar points,
a grey felt hat tilted back off the head,
the face vulturine, eyes which have stepped in
to live with mental space and monitor

all drifting fractal implosions.
The man is easy in his Kansas yard,
his GHQ since 1982,
the New York bunker left behind, and cats
flopping around his feet, finding the sun,
picking up on psi energies.

He's waiting for extraterrestrials,
psychic invasion; we can bypass death
by shooting interplanetary serum.
Some of us are the deathless ones. He pours
a crippling slug of Jack Daniels.
The body can't function without toxins
or weird metabolic fluctuations.
He's waiting for the big event.

And has become a legend, now a myth,
a cellular mythologem.
His double's pressure-locked in the psyche,
for fear he blows a fuse, goes out on leave
and kills. He is invaded by Genet,
his presence asks for love, for completion.
The man wanders to his tomato patch;
his amanuensis snatches a break.

The light is hazy gold. He'll outlive death,
be here when there's no longer a planet.

ARTHUR RIMBAUD

THE DRUNKEN BOAT
(Le Bateau ivre)

No longer guided by haulers, I felt
the current chase me down sluggish rivers.
Yelping redskins had made human targets,
nailed them to stakes and cut out their livers.

I was indifferent to every crew,
carriers of English cottons, Flemish wheat.
My haulers dead, the uproars extinguished,
the waters left me to a steady beat.

Last winter, more dumbstruck than a child's mind
I ran into the ferocious rip-tides.
The surf lashed me; loosened peninsulas
were like white thunder smashing at my sides.

The storm celebrated my sea vigils.
Lighter than a cork I danced on the waves,
the big rollers which distribute the drowned.
Ten nights. Lighthouses marking sailors' graves.

Sweeter than waspish apples to children,
the green water oozed through my pinewood hull,
scouring the vomit splashes and blue wine.
Rudder and planks were gashed by a sea-bull.

Later, I found the Poem of the Sea,
infused with starlight and latescent spray,
and nosed through green azure where a drowned man
rolled up and down and sometimes seemed to stay.

It's there, the bitter red of love ferments,
stronger than alcohol, madder than lyres,
slow rhythms heard around the break of day
light up the deep blue with delirium's fires.

I've known skies split by lightnings, waterspouts,
surf and the looping currents, evening too,
and dawn exalted like a flock of doves.
I've seen the things man thought he saw and knew.

I've watched the low sun packed with mystic scars,
its long violet clots burning out in space,
resembling manic actors on the boards,
waves running blinds up across the surface.

I've dreamt of a green night with dazzled snows,
a kiss rising from the deeps to the sky,
the circulation of all unknown saps,
yellow and blue phosphor singing in the sea's eye.

I've followed in gestative months the swell
running like hysterical cows to smash
their violent panic on the reefs. I've sensed
the snouting sea-herd stilled by a star's flash.

I've struck against amazing Floridas
where flowers are panther's eyes in human skin,
and rainbows dropped down as the bridle reins
keeping the glaucous sea-horizons in.

I've seen enormous swamps ferment, fish traps
where a Leviathan rots on the beach.
Water avalanching out of a calm,
cataracts shrieking in their overreach!

Glaciers, silver suns, waves shot through red,
I've seen wrecks in brown gulfs, stood upside-down,
and giant serpents devoured by vermin
smoke with black scent in a knotted tree crown.

I should have liked to point out to children
gold dolphins singing as they broke the wave,
while spindrift flowers jostled my driftings,
and winds beat like wings over the sea's grave.

Sometimes a victim, coursing between poles,
the sea whose groundswell lifted with the breeze
carried black flowers with yellow suckers
and dragged me like a woman on her knees . . .

Almost an island, with its squalling birds
high over beaches, I rocked on the deep,
or sailed on, seeing through my smashed rigging
drowned men somersault backwards into sleep.

I ran, a boat conversant with sea-caves,
blasted by the storm into birdless air;
I whose sodden boards, taking in water,
would have attracted no one to its flare.

Free, smoking and risen from violet fogs,
I who bored through the red sky like a wall
carried preserves for good poets, blue jam,
azure snot, sunlight fattened to a ball.

I shot, speckled with small electric moons,
a wild plank, black sea-horses by my side,
while July furnaced down burning funnels
and ultramarine skies fumed in the tide . . .

I who trembled, hearing on the skyline,
rampant Behemoths, a whirlpool's shut eye,
spun on blue spaces, longing for Europe,
its parapets crowding into the sky.

I've seen spiral galaxies and islands
whose delirious skies open out to death.
And from those bottomless nights, golden birds,
will you rise at last on the future's breath?

But truly I've known too much pain. The dawns
are inconsolable, the moon a scar,
love's left me disconnected, spaced on drugs,
I need to sink rock bottom, go that far.

If there's one water in Europe I need,
it's the black cold pool where a child will try
sometimes at evening to launch a toy boat,
its structure lighter than a butterfly.

I can no longer, lit up by the surf,
sit in the wake of cotton boats, nor keep
appointment with riotous flags, nor dive
under prison ships steering for the deep.

A new translation by Jeremy Reed

GEORGII VLASENKO

DEAD BIRDS OF RUSSIA

greetings, my brothers — dead birds,
white bones, your unburied remains,
wings, broken fans, lost gloves,
feathers, wreckage of rowboats and sailboats
tossed up on the shore after storms.
without gravestones or memorials,
caught in a thicket of heather and blackthorn,
hugging the earth in a final embrace,
compressed like papier-mâché by the silence,
you have made yourselves familiars of the black earth,
the plowed field,
the stricken leaves.

Icaruses! the air would make way with a whistle
when you performed your dizzying somersaults
and caught your sinking heart mid-flight
as it fell like a pea from your breast.
the elements molded you, shaped you, polished you
like the sea patiently nurturing a grain of sand
into a pearl and a horned shell,
the rose, ear and lips of the ocean.
the middle-aged mill operator stares
in awe at the sinuous mother-of-pearl —
he thought he had mastered
the deepest secrets of the lathe.

coral and skeleton of the same mold,
the same casting. under the flesh the arches, the notochords,
supporting these vaults the pilasters of tibiae —
what were the hammers and anvils whose sounds they absorbed?
dry land, and everything dwelling thereon,
set between sea and sky, almost

like a slice of cheese in a sandwich.
wings on the moss's dark green shot with black,
the breastbone a gleaming white wedge
(a boat asleep, its nose burrowed in the sand), —
a jeweler's handiwork, surely, in a display case.

birds of Russia's fields and plains,
no funereal march accompanies your final passage,
no relatives or hired mourners arrive to shed tears,
no orator is there to rattle off a speech, to say,
"Rest in peace, dear friend, and may the earth
lie light as feather down upon you."
you are yourselves partly of down,
and so the wind draws your remains lightly
into its currents, where they are crushed,
ground to powder by the millstones of heaven
and circle the earth, light, wisps of smoke,
until they find rest in the great woodlands
awaiting new incarnations as kingfishers,
plovers and goldfinches.

you are no more subject to the vicissitudes
of fate and weather. the cold of hungry winters
will not drop its tomtits, bullfinches, sparrows,
as a clumsy novice who lets the vigil lamp fall.
covered with stricken leaves and frostbitten pine needles,
you have finally been granted your freedom
from frost and serfdom.
do not remove the red berry from the beak
of the dead bird. come spring
the dogrose will blossom over the body.

my brothers, you slept in stations,
on benches, suitcases and duffelbags,
standing in lines in the foodstores with sacks.
the doormen kept you out of their hotels
and restaurants. full up, they said, no vacancies,
reserved for foreigners.
you ate slop in the cafeterias,

and working up a sweat, you daydreamed on the bathhouse benches,
birching your taciturn backs,
starlings, crakes, drakes.

in freight cars, on plank beds,
you travelled to the city, my gutsy sisters,
to push rollers across newly laid asphalt,
to break up the road-ice with picks,
to work in the kitchens of the privileged.
what rays of light did you see in the drinks
downed on holidays, birthdays and wakes?
my mothers, you met my fathers
too early, and they threw you off too soon.
after thousands of washloads
and hundreds of bags of potatoes,
you lay down on hospital beds,
sacrificing yourselves to the utmost
to raise up sons and daughters
you did not attend premieres.
you slept standing up in crowded commuter trains.
your faces untouched by cosmetics and dripping with sweat
gleamed like the lamp on a miner's helmet.

bluejays, pigeons, turtledoves,
your shoulders scraped raw by the barge-hauler's strap,
lining the White Sea canals with your selves,
nameless voices from the blue chorus,
you were poured into the roar of dams
where banks were flooded over.
Nizhnii, Tver, Simbirsk, Tsaritsyn —
cities that are no more —
remember your long and mournful songs.
their current sometimes flows
into the polyphony of the choir, setting the tongues
of candles to sway in the chandeliers.
the more I think of Russia, the more
I want to cry, o birds of Russia's expanses,
geese, swans, orioles.

Translated by Ron Vroon

ANDREI CODRESCU

AM MYTH: WHAZZIT, WHOZZIT, WHOZINONIT?

Considering myth one has to stand before the word for a moment: there is capital M Myth which is the kind of story that never changes, was, is, and will be; a story written by no one but told by everyone; a story that exists independently of its tellers; a story that cannot be changed by temporal circumstances; the elements of it may be updated, the language of it may be hipped, but the story stays the same.

Creation stories are myths of this type. "In the beginning was the Word," or "In the Beginning was Spider Woman," are stories that cannot be changed because they describe the activities of divine beings in the *illo tempore*, before history began. The actions of the gods at that time before time were completely significant and irreversibly generative. A gesture once made set worlds in motion. The description of that activity, carried into history by story tellers, had the function of abolishing time and putting its listeners or re-enacters in a sacred time, outside history, in the *illo tempore* of the original divine activity.

The founding myths of nations belong to this category. The founding myth of Romania is Mioritza, the story of a love affair between a boy and a sheep. Most nations were founded, incidentally, by bestiality, incest, or some kind of taboo mix of humans and animals. Romans arrived in history on a stream of wolf's milk. We Romanians have sheep fucking at the founding of our nationhood. This boy, a shepherd, was warned by his lover, the sheep Mioritza, of an impending plan by his two older brothers to kill him in the morning, in order to steal his sheep. The boy, characteristically for this culture, does not take precautions. He does not hide, run away, or get up in the middle of the night to kill his brothers first. Au contraire, he accepts his fate. But he tells Mioritza to go to his mother after he is killed and to tell her that he didn't really die, that he had married the moon instead, and that all the stars had been at his wedding. He then proceeds to describe each star — in case his mother wants to know details. He explains where every star came from and what its story is.

In other words, he offers the cosmogony of the Romanian sky. After he is killed, Mioritza wanders, telling the story over and over. The path of the wandering of the forlorn sheep is the natural border of Romania: a moving border from the mountains to the sea, a story-telling border.

In the Americas, the world before the white man was woven by a spider. But modern America, the white man's America, was born in history not in pre-history, so we have no gods. The God on the dollar bill is an eyeball, the eye of a camera, watching everything with the relative objectivity of science for which everything is equally significant. There is no *illo tempore* where the founding gestures continue unchanged. In fact, change is the only unchanging law.

"What does not change/is the will to change," said Charles Olson, a very big man and poet of oceanic verse, who sought to create an epic poem, "Maximus," that would contain both the founding mythology of America and its subsequent history.

Olson took the little town of Gloucester and proceeded to verbalise and dramatise it beginning with the geology of its rocks and the stories the Atlantic Ocean bequeathed to her fishermen. In employing the ocean, Olson borrowed shamelessly from the Greeks and the Phoenicians, sea-faring people whose stories he found still agitating the foam. That was a bit of American disingenuity and brilliance: the poetic ocean is naturally made from all the stories told about it and almost all stories spring from the ocean. Dipping into it for myth is like shooting fish in a barrel, to mix a couple of containers. But in appropriating the myths for American use, Olson did that most American of activities: collage.

American myth is collage, as is just about everything else in America, except geography. Collage is the medium, par excellence, of our cultural story. We are a collage of cultures. Our story-telling is produced today by television, a collage medium. Our language is the language of images, which are collageable items. Myth-dipped Europeans sick of history set up America as a collage of their utopian yearnings. Here was paradise, streets paved with gold, dogs with pretzels on their tails — my grandmother's version — , fertile soil, unlimited horizons, rivers of ale, mountains of salt. America, for immigrants, was post-history, which is the same as pre-history. In European myths, everything happened at the beginning. In America, everything was going to happen in the end, in the future. Paradise and utopia met here and paved over the prehistory of the original inhabitants.

Every myth is the story of a quest: the hero overcomes the horrendous obstacles of temporality (or history) in order to find eternity (or utopia). For the Europeans, there was no Original Sin in America. All that stayed behind in Europe. America was Utopia, the end of the Quest, possible because the Old had been left behind. This particular belief gave birth to another kind of myth. This is the sort of story that exists in a cluster of similar stories that form a "mythology" or a "mythography." Its salient feature is that it has been manufactured by a myth-making industry, Broadway, Hollywood, or Madison Avenue. The raw material of it was the yearning of immigrants faced with the challenges of American space.

The most enduring — relatively speaking — myths of this provenance are: in America you can start again; you can change your name and your face and be re-born; hard work (or luck) not history, is what matters; in America everything is possible; the rewards of puritanism is hedonism; paradise is here and now — as the Oneida community and the Living Theatre told us — ; we are mechanically gifted and will find a technological solution to everything.

We have a constitutional right to the "pursuit of happiness," which has now become "the relentless pursuit of happiness." In the beginning was the automated kitchen and the computer. Everything about America has to do with beginnings. We have no eschatology, no science of the end. In the afterlife, we begin again, just as if we were moving from New York to California. Our White Goddess is the refrigerator: she stands white and tall in the kitchen, drawing all, feared by all, giver of sustenance and source of fearful calories.

Some of the heroes of these American myths, or mechano-mythography, are: the loner who conquers evil through grit and charm, the cowboy with a heart of gold, the whore with the rapier wit, the maladjusted emigrant who renews himself (me), the "destroyer of worlds," — Oppenheimer or Teller — , and the Giver of Meaning, Vanna White.

Edward Teller and Vanna White, to take only two of these mechano-archetypes, represent two permanent features of the American soul: the male part that desires bigger and bigger explosions indifferently of cost, and the nurturing female who proves time after time that there is meaning in a meaningless universe, that there really are words, phrases, and things, in the lacunae between disconnected letters. The American quest, as exemplified by these two archetypes, is for a bright afterlife where meaning is guaranteed. Of course, we have to first surrender doubt and then die. This myth would not function if we refused to blow up or, at least, entertained some suspicion that behind the jumble of letters lies a Finnish word or, horror of horrors, a Dada word.

Edward Teller and Vanna White have no equivalents in ancient myth. She is a blond native born of the California imaging fields, and is a collage of many myths. She is a little bit like Isis who searched for the fourteen pieces of the body of Osiris and gathered them back together. This she does, not with a man, but with language, every night, on television. She is a little bit like Arachne, the girl famous in Greece for her skill at weaving. But there is no Athena to become jealous of her because Vanna has a good contract that protects her from just such contingencies.

Edward Teller is a collage, too. A Hungarian Jew who suffered the loss of a leg in pre-war Germany, he developed the hydrogen bomb and was the father of the Star Wars program. In Europe his physical and mythical M.O. would have reminded everyone of the Wandering Jew, Mephistopheles, and Dr. Faustus. A bum leg is always the Devil's mark. But in America, Dr. Teller became an American myth: the god of technological pre-eminence based on the joy of apocalyptic fire.

Note the names: Vanna White, white, white, whiter than Snow White, who has whited-out ambiguity, whitened the darkness of meaninglessness and chaos. And Teller, the teller of the story that begins in the darkness of medieval Europe and ends in the paradise of utopian America. The teller of the End and the White of the afterlife are myths of technology, American myths.

If one understands now the distinction between immutable myth and mutable myth-making by American myth-machines, I would like to introduce a third category of myth: artist-generated paradoxes whose function is to sabotage techno-myths.

Ezra Pound, said to Americans in American: "Make it new!" And that has been the imperative for all those who would generate an idea, a story or an object. That was the mythical modern imperative. The paradox is that you cannot create a new myth of the *illo tempore* variety I mentioned earlier. You can only collage bits of existing myth in order to fabricate an operating story. And that's the story of the modern, from Cubism and Joyce's *Ulysses*, to Teller and Vanna.

One can argue that Vanna is post-modern but post-modernism, to me, is only a stylistic turn of the modern: the collaging imperative is the same, with the added adagio: "Get it used!." In other words, "Make it new" has suffered the necessary corrective, "Get it used," making it not just accurate but chic to use used materials. And the more used — the more ancient — the better. "Use-value" is the post-modern recognition that we needn't fool anyone: that the machinery of the illusion is chic and valuable, equally as "real" as the myth, object, or story.

Artist-generated collages become generalised cultural myths when they get big distribution. After that, they become automatic, generic received ideas with varying half-lives that float in the national psyche until they burn out. The machinery of illusion is a giant maw that needs artists' creations at an increasing rate. The mythical contest being currently played out is between the speed of the artist and the speed of the machine that would employ his or her stories. We have to make faster and faster to keep ahead of the dragon chasing us. Because once he catches us that's the end of any light at the end of the tunnel. *The machine prolongs the tunnel — into infinity*. And you can't turn around to run away either, because at the beginning of the tunnel is Mr. Teller, with the H-bomb in his hand, and at the end is Vanna, turning the letters.

In America, immutable myth, mechano-myth, and artist myth, have to deal with one element which may or may not be purely American: Space. Charles Olson begins his discussion of Melville with this assertion: "Space is the central fact of man in North America." We have done our best to technologically abolish space, and to banish the very ideas of the "outside." Yet, American space is what all our stories are about: the East-West journey, the vastness of the prairie, the marshes, the flood plains, the journey of the Mississippi.

Space is the one immutable — no matter how much we have tried to move it outside of our perception — character of our myth, mythography, and artistry.

New Orleans, May 10, 1994

STEVE KOWIT

MARILYN

"Marilyn's death was one of those news events about which you can remember how you heard it, where you heard it and how you felt."
— Charles Champlin, *L.A. Times*

As the Brighton Local screeched through its tunnels,
— those lurid yellow epileptic lights
blinking overhead like fitfull sleep — I'd doze uneasily,
& wake a dozen times before that filthy subway
lurching thru the dark squealed into Brooklyn Heights,
where I'd emerge, dazed as Dante back from Hell,
the summer morning soberingly bright.
I was all jangled nerves — unsexed, frayed, disconcerted.
Still, had she greeted me those mornings
with the sleepy languor of a woman rising from bed,
we might have become the passionate lovers we had intended.
Instead, she'd be bustling about the kitchen
finishing her husband's breakfast dishes, cleaning
up her six year old's spilled egg. Instead of making love,
we'd end up at that table giggling over everything,
like kids — Dr. Benway, Fidel's beard, Paul Rep's
little book of zen tales we both loved.
I was too shy, I guess, to take her in my arms: waltz her
over to the couch. unzip our morning reticence.
However far crosstown her husband's office was,
it was too close for comfort.
                              "I guess it isn't working,
is it, Steven?" she volunteered out of the blue,
one morning, with one of those annunciatory sighs.
— & I said "No. . . . no, I guess it isn't." Though it wasn't true:
As far I knew, everything had been okay — I mean
things take time. Whatever we would be to one another

had been just beginning.
She stood, as I recall it, by the window,
bathed in that angelic summer light, freckled & tomboyish
with those mischievous bright eyes
cast toward the street, the curtain just behind her, billowing.
Before her son was born, she went on quietly, her breasts
had been a good deal fuller . . . She wished, she said,
we had known each other back then.
I was embarrassed, of course — & didn't know what to say.
Her breasts? Was that it, then? And had we failed each other
in some way? Or was that simply just a way of getting out
of saying something else that might have been more hurtful
to have said? My own guess, looking back on that occasion
in my life so many years ago, is that our lack of passion
had more to do with that long, sobering subway ride
into Brooklyn, & with our conflicted intentions, & our guilt —
she was, after all, a woman with a husband & son.
Though at this point there isn't any way to figure any of this
out. I mean that sort of thing is always complex & confusing.
That was thirty years ago & I was just a kid,
oblivious, full of dreams, self-obsessed.
Two or three evenings later, Marilyn dropped in at my place
in Manhattan with a pretty girlfriend, introducing us,
as if to say you two would make a lovely couple. . . .
& that was that. I never saw her again.
You know how sometimes you think about old friends,
wondering how things turned out for them,
or if they're even still alive.
Had we not been so young, our friendship
would not have ended so stupidly, I think.
Two weeks or so before we parted, Marilyn & I
had caught the subway to Naponsett Beach, & getting off
the train I'd picked up a discarded New York *Mirror* —
one of those awful tabloids full of lurid photos,
where we'd read, in shock, that Marilyn Monroe
had killed herself in a motel room.
My recollection is that things, if only for a moment,
became immensely vivid, the way one squints

stepping out of a movie house into the astonishingly
bright light of an ordinary afternoon, so that
for two or three moments that harsh, painful brilliance
is both thrilling & difficult to move through.
But then again it might have only been the glare
of that early afternoon in August by the ocean that
I'm misremembering, & have gotten mixed up with my feelings.
— You know how it is when such a day detaches
itself from the days around it. Which is why, I suppose,
I imagine that I remember it with such clarity,
I mean considering how long ago it was,
how at one moment, lying there together on the beach,
she looked at me with that exquisite, gaminlike expression,
& I bent my body slowly into hers
& pressed my lips against her mouth. Believe me,
all too well I understand that life is gone
& that this poem is nothing but a paltry reconstruction
of desire, fugitive & half-connected images,
& tenderness for my own history — the offspring
of my longing to reclaim that woman who, one day — not knowing
what to say or think — I'd stupidly let vanish from my life,
being, as I have indicated, painfully young
& ignorant & self-obsessed.
You know as well as I how hopelessly confused
such memories, in time, are apt to be. Everything,
that blanket's musty scent, the coco-butter oil of her flesh,
the pungent seawrack, & that irresistible & mischievous
expression in her eyes as I bent down
to brush my lips against her lips, may well
be all mixed up with wishful thinking, poetry, conventions
of contemporary discourse, everything
that's happened to me since. Some poor
lost creature who was sexy, famous, rich, took pills
& killed herself. The sun that day ablaze
above the North Atlantic shelf. Naponsett Beach. The scorching
sand, both painful & delicious. Intimations of the infinite.
Those breakers, with their dark, percussive bass.

LAURA STORTONI

To Sylvia Plath, Ann Sexton, Alfonsina Storni,
Antonia Pozzi, Marina Tsvetayeva, Virginia Woolf
and Ingrid Jonker,

An Angry Requiem

Do not feel safe. The poet remembers.
You can kill one, but another is born.
The words are written down, the deed, the date.
— Czeslaw Milosz

If the best woman poets
want only to die,
and take their lives,
      yearning
for the embrace of the earth
as warm and moist
as our wombs

Then
who will be left
to carry the pain
on muscular shoulders
for the sisters who are now
in the cradle?

We think sometimes —
when loneliness bites our liver
with its sharp beak —
that it would be easy
to float away, new Ophelias
on a streaming bed of water-lilies, or
to get ourselves to a nunnery
where the pain is lulled
by the anaesthesia of God and the Blessed Virgin.

But then
who would be left
for the non-virgins of tomorrow, for the less
courageous of today?

Don't let yourself
float away. Get thee to the rocky shore.

BARRY GIFFORD

THE END OF RACISM

One of my favorite places to go when I was a kid in Chicago was Riverview, the giant amusement park on the North Side. Riverview, which during the 1950s was nicknamed Polio Park, after the reigning communicable disease of the decade, had dozens of rides, including some or the fastest, most terrifying roller coasters ever designed. Among them were The Silver Streak, The Comet, The Wild Mouse, The Flying Turns, and The Bobs. Of these, The Flying Turns, a seatless ride that lasted all of thirty seconds or so and required the passengers in each car to recline consecutively on one another, was my favorite. The Turns did not operate on tracks but rather on a steeply banked, bobsled-like series of tortuous sliding curves that never failed to engender in me the sensation of being about to catapult out of the car over the stand of trees to the west of the parking lot. To a fairly manic kid, which I was, this was a big thrill, and I must have ridden The Flying Turns hundreds of times between the ages of seven and sixteen.

The Bobs, however, was the most frightening roller coaster in the park. Each year several people were injured or killed on that ride; usually when a kid attempted to prove his bravery by standing up in the car at the apex of the first long, slow climb, and was then flipped out of the car as it jerked suddenly downward at about a hundred miles per hour. The kids liked to speculate about how many lives The Bobs had taken over the years. I knew only one kid, Earl Weyerholz, who claimed to have stood up in his car at the top of the first hill more than once and lived to tell about it. I never doubted Earl Weyerholz because I once saw him put his arm up to the biceps into an aquarium containing two piranhas just to recover a quarter Bobby DiMarco had thrown into it and dared Earl to go after. Earl was eleven then. He died in 1958, at the age of fourteen, from the more than two hundred bee stings he sustained that year at summer camp in Wisconsin. How or why he got stung so often was never explained to me. I just assumed somebody had dared him to stick his arms into a few hives for a dollar or something.

Shoot the Chutes was also a popular Riverview ride. Passengers rode in boats that slid at terrific speed into a pool and everybody got soaking wet. The Chutes never really appealed very much to me, though; I never saw the point of getting wet for no good reason. The Parachute was another one that did not thrill me. Being dropped to the ground from a great height while seated on a thin wooden plank with only a narrow metal bar to hold onto was not my idea of a good time. In fact, just the thought of it scared the hell out of me; I didn't even like to watch people do it. I don't think my not wanting to go on The Parachute meant that I was acrophobic, however, because I was extremely adept at scaling garage roofs by the drainpipes in the alleys and jumping from one roof to the next. The Parachute just seemed like a crazy thing to submit oneself to; as did The Rotor, a circular contraption that spun around so fast that when the floor was removed riders were plastered to the walls by centrifugal force. Both The Parachute and The Rotor always had long lines of people waiting to be exquisitely tortured.

What my friends and I were most fond of at Riverview was Dunk the Nigger. At least that's what we called the concession where by throwing a baseball at a target on a handle and hitting it square you could cause the seat lever in the attached cage to release and plunge the man sitting on the perch into a tank of about five feet of water. All of the guys who worked in the cages were black, and they hated to see us coming. Between the ages of thirteen and sixteen my friends and I terrorized these guys. They were supposed to taunt the thrower, make fun of him or her and try to keep them spending quarters for three balls. Most people who played this game were lucky to hit the target hard enough to dunk the clown once in every six tries; but my buddies and I became experts. We'd buy about ten dollars worth of baseballs and keep these guys going down, time after time.

Of course they hated us with a passion. "Don't you little motherfuckers have somewhere else to go?" they'd yell. "Goddam motherfuckin' whiteboy, I'm gon' get yo' ass when I gets my break!" We'd just laugh and keep pegging hardballs at the trip lever targets. My pal Big Steve was great at Dunk the Nigger; he was our true ace because he threw the hardest and his arm never got tired. "You fat ofay sumbitch!" one of the black guys would shout at Big Steve as he dunked him for the fifth pitch in a row. "Stop complaining," Steve would yell back at him. "You're getting a free bath, aren't ya?"

None of us thought too much about the fact that the job of taunt-and-dunk was about half a cut above being a carnival geek and a full cut below working at a car wash. It never occurred to us, more than a quarter of a century ago, why it was that all of the guys on the perches were black, or that we were racists. Unwitting racists, perhaps; after all, we were kids, ignorant and foolish products of White Chicago during the 1950s.

One summer afternoon in 1963, the year I turned sixteen, my friends and I arrived at Riverview and headed straight for Dunk the Nigger. We were shocked to see a white guy sitting on a perch in one of the cages. Nobody said anything but we all stared at him. Big Steve bought some balls and began hurling them at one of the black guys' target. "What's the matter, gray?" the guy shouted at Steve. "Don't want to pick on one of your own?"

I don't remember whether or not I bought any balls that day, but I do know it was the last time I went to the concession. In fact, that was one of the last times I patronized Riverview, since I left Chicago early the following year and Riverview was torn down not long after. I don't know what Big Steve or any of my other old friends who played Dunk the Nigger with me think about it now, or even if they've ever thought about it at all.

That's just the way things were.

Lawrence Ferlinghetti   *This Is Not A Man*, 1994

AMIRI BARAKA

THE X IS BLACK

If the fire catch
    fire, & an X
    burn in, that X is Black
    & leaves an
    empty space. It
    is that place
    where we live
    the Afro-American
    Nation.

If the flag
    catch afire
    & an X burn in
    the only stripes is
    on our back
    the only star
    blown free
    in the northern sky
    no red but our
    blood, no white
    but slavers and Klux in robes
    no blue
    but our songs

If the flag catch fire
    & an X
    burn in

that X is black
& the space that is left
is our history
now a mystery

we only live
where the flag
is not
where the air is funky
the music
hot
Inside the hole
in the American soul
that space, that place
empty of democracy
we live
inside the burned boundaries
of a wasted symbol
X humans, X slaves, unknown, incorrect
crossed out, multiplying the wealth of others

If the flag
      catch fire
      & an X burn in
      that X
      believe me,
      is black.

ALBERTO SAVINIO

"Arthur Schopenhauer was so unhappy with the history of philosophy that he created a history of philosophy for himself and for his own personal use; I am so unhappy with encyclopedias that I wrote an encyclopedia for *my*self and for *my* own personal use."

— A.S.

Hitler

In September 1943 I was in Versilia. Cavalcades of Germans in camouflage dress and soldiers disguised as toads were neatly invading our most "Italian" cities, and were spreading like colossal iron caterpillars over our most tranquil fields. At noon on September 11, I crossed the marble fortress of Piazza Vittoria Apuana, stopping to quench my thirst at a little stand in which a woman was selling cold drinks and slices of watermelon. A young bicyclist, arriving unexpectedly, said to her, "Have you heard? They say Hitler is dead." The woman continued to mix the almond syrup and the crushed ice, but displayed neither astonishment nor any other feeling. The young cyclist, a bit offended, repeated his possibly false news two or three times. Finally, faced with the woman's persistent indifference, he and I eyed each other conspiratorially, sharing the extraordinary realization that *she had never heard of Hitler.* In 1936, on the occasion of a lynx-hunt near the Pinsk marshes which was organized by the Polish Republic in honor of Hermann Goering, it became clear that the residents of that desolate region were absolutely unaware of the war *par excellence* that we had called the Great War, but which had never even reached their vicinity. Several years ago in southern Naples, I met a woman who in her entire life had yet to receive a letter or even a postcard. But the woman from Vittoria Apuana was neither old nor a native of the Pinsk marshes; she was still young and vigorous, and she lived in one of the most civilized and enlightened areas in Italy. What should we conclude from this? It occurred to me that she was ignorant of Hitler's existence *for hygienic reasons*, and the usefulness of this notion helped me to overcome its absurdity. I remembered that, many years before, I myself had proposed the foundation of a league whose members were sworn to ignore Mussolini and never to speak his name. If more people were to exhibit the will, the steadfastness, and, above all, the "hygienic care" necessary to respect the vow of a similar league, it would be as impossible for men like Mussolini and Hitler to rise as it would a balloon in an airless room. Why is the widespread observance of similar vows impossible? Because men like Hitler and Mussolini represent, express and embody the ideas, the desires, and the ambitions of a great majority of men — that is to say, ideas of military glory, desire for domination, ambition and conquest. Why be shocked and lament the consequences of a Mussolini's or a Hitler's power when men, *all men*, are educated to the same ideas of "greatness" of which Hitler and Mussolini are the precise expression? Although, even here, some striking exceptions do exist. From my earliest childhood until now that I have lived more than half a century, I have always resisted, I have always held in profound contempt the qualities that comprise the "greatness" and the "glory" of men like Alexander, like Caesar, like Napoleon, like Hitler, like Mussolini. The mistake lies in separating the "types" who succeed from those who fail. It is not a question of renouncing Mussolini or Hitler when they, in decline, no longer provide what people "expect from them." It is a question of transforming the attitudes that *uphold* these "types"; it is a question of abolishing the ideas that render men like Hitler not only conceivable but *passionately desired*. It is a question, finally, of a radical change in the concept of greatness. Within those who do not see a sign — even in their own hearts — of the misery that the "greatness" of these types has caused us. It is rather the danger that, while mending the damages of Hitler and Mussolini, we have created new Hitlers and new Mussolinis. But who will warn us of this danger?

Translated from the Italian by Susan Etlinger

Translator's Note: The entries in Alberto Savinio's *New Encyclopedia*, published by Adelphi Edizioni in 1977, originally appeared in the Italian review *Domus* between January 1941 and October 1942, as well as in Italian newspapers such as *La Stampa* and *Corriere della Sera* throughout the forties.

ALBERTO SAVINIO   113

MARK TERRILL

Bukowski: 3/10/94

I was sitting at my desk
working on a poem
when my wife came in
with the news
"Bukowski died"
I put down my pen
and leaned back
remembering how I
used to read his column
"Notes of a Dirty Old Man"
in the *L.A. Free Press*
long before anybody had
ever even heard of Bukowski
and how I once saw his face
that gnarly freakish thing
on the cover of a book
not knowing who it was
and picked it up
just for that reason
only to discover
it was the same guy
whose column I'd been
reading all those years
and there in those pages
was a world not unlike
my own, that same constellation
of booze, broads, and despair
and I figured if he could do it
I could do it too
so I bought a second-hand typer
started writing poems and
sending them around

got published in *Vagabond*
along with Bukowski
a simple little thing
about the fifty cent movies
but the point of the matter is
I probably never would have
written a single fucking poem
if it wasn't for that guy
More than anyone else
he proved that poetry
didn't have to be an
academic thing, or
strictly for sissies
or phonetic windbags
that it was something
that could be lived
and felt and understood
as real as that cheap red wine
as real as those bills
piled up in the mailbox
as real as that landlady
hounding you for the rent
as real as those shit jobs
and crazy fucked up women
as real as hangovers and
the blazing Los Angeles sun
as real as anything at all
Then I let that feeling
that had been lurking inside me
for the last couple of days,
as if I'd somehow *known*,
come up over me and
culminate in my chest
accompanied by a long, hard
lump in my throat and a
certain sogginess of the eyes
surprising even myself
And then that sudden acknowledgment

of irreplaceable loss that
came hammering down
When all the good people are gone
who will be left?
But why all these feelings
of tenderness and sorrow
for some pock-marked old geezer
who wrote dirty books laden
with great existential insights
whom I never even met?
Then it became apparent
in a frightening sort of way
that there are the
Great Living Poets
the Great Dead Poets
and then there's me
another two-bit guttersnipe
with a word-processor
and literary ambitions
of the burning kind
forever in debt to
a dirty old man
whom I never even knew
and I leaned forward
picked up my pen
and went back to work.

There's so much to do.

Buk, we'll miss you
like a son of a bitch.

Right

Don't ask me what happened
I had some kind of attack
and went into a McDonald's
on Edgeware road in London
employees so pale
you could almost
see through them
the blacks over here
the whites over there
no one can read the
no smoking sign
and one table away
sits a couple
both about my age
but with a baby
in a stroller that
keeps getting in the way
she's leaning over her
Big Mac and fries
driving home a point
eventually
breaking into tears
he's rubbing his face
and looking out the window
in quiet desperation
which makes me think
she must be right
I'm sipping my coffee
the forlorn observer
removed but aware
watching them
going down the street now
leaning into the
wind and rain
she drying her eyes

he flipping up his collar
the baby
doomed.

Sand

Leaving the Hotel du Nord
in little Algeria
and heading down
the Rue de Clignancourt
to the Hotel Idéal
Tuesday morning
the city doing
what it always does
charming
annoying
attracting
repelling
the street is
all torn up
from construction
and during the night
the rain has washed
a big pile of sand
all the way down the hill
to the Rue Poulet
where on the corner
stands a man
gray hair and glasses
T-shirt and paunch
shabby suit coat
and a wooden cane
he's sorting through
a handful of old
lottery tickets
about to throw them away

hesitating
pursing his lips
looking around with
that despondent look
that catches me and
everything else
in its wake and
washes us all
further down
the street.

The Rebel

Two days
before Christmas
in Hamburg
evening gliding in
behind the TV tower
the dusk peppered
with snowflakes
Mother and son
meet on the sidewalk
she looks old and tired
he looks to be about ten
she's berating him
dumping on him
driving her point home
while he studies
the sidewalk
hands in his pockets
kicking at nothing
waiting patiently
until she's done
But there are more
ploys and threats
How heavy and sinister

can Christmas be?
Then she's finished
and he walks away
his head still down
mumbling in agreement
while she gets in
the last word
Then, she too, turns
and continues on
waddling between
her shopping bags
smug with satisfaction
Then, suddenly
half way down the block
he stops, looks back
yells something
indecipherable
does a little dance
turns again
and runs.

INGEBORG TEUFFENBACH

3 POEMS

*dedicated to my son Fritjof Capra in grateful
memory of the first Week in May 1992*

Devon

to capture
not with the camera
but with the eyes
THE SONG OF THE EARTH
reddish-brown
its inner lights
turned outward
home for anyone
who enters here
thin-skinned

Dartmoor

stone walls stone blocks
stone houses
floodgates of light
horizons
drawn with charcoal
wild horses galloping
where from — where to?
the whirl of life hollowed out
wind-blown

River Dart

liberated
from settlements and
concrete walls
he flows back to the
verdant mossy veils
of silent banks

what have they done
to his brothers
that they are no longer allowed
to mirror
blue duck feathers and
black wood

a sound detaches itself
from the octave of
memories
a longing for
childhood

KAYE MCDONOUGH

THE SIN

Pregnant I feel like a walking aquarium
the creature inside me flipping
    like some marvelous fish!
One day he'll beach to strange new shores
    where catty predators wait
    with nets of morality

This coming nativity my mother sees as Doomsday
"But you're not married! Pity the poor child!
    Think of the neighbors!"
She wails tearily into the phone Bible stories
    of the Woman at the Well
while I long to set sail like Noah in his Ark

The man who made this life in me
    knows it is holy
creation sinless as a midnight sea
As for me, I know I have cast my bread
    wide upon the waters
Let only the fishes of the sea
    bear witness against me

1984

JAMES LAUGHLIN

The Immanence of Your Body

It's nearly three years since we've
   been together,
Since we made love.
The circumstances of life have kept
   us apart.
But tonight as I sit here in half-darkness,
Listening to the *Four Last Songs*,
Remembering things about you,
I'm convinced of the immanence,
   the indwelling,
Of your body in mine.
You're a part of me again.
I feel your every touch.
I can feel the warm pressure of the flow
Of your bloodstream against mine.
I pray that my body is equally
   immanent in yours,
That we have not heard our last song.

The Love Beast

is a creature of rare beauty
she appears to be gentle and herbivorous
she inhabits green pastures
she nibbles watercress
but beware: at certain seasons
or when the moon is full,
the love beast may become carnivorous,
and her favorite dish is a poet.

For the unfortunate bard
there is only one protection:
he must confect a sonnet so sizzling,
or a tercet so toasty,
that the love beast will frizzle her gullet
and flee to the marshes
to assuage her amorous pain.

HOWARD HART

Old Puerto Vallarta

There was that moment
                    forgotten now
When water was pure
And stars were in the air
                    at night
                    not blotted out
                    by the exhaust
                    from cars
I miss them too much
                    the stars
The vast void black I see
                    around the moon
                    frightens me
I remember once from the back of
                    a wagon
             over a cobblestone
             street in Mexico
How the Van Gogh
                    vision and I
                    were one for once
With the sky full of animals
                    and gold phosphor lamps

NANOS VALAORITIS

A Spaghetti-Western
Co-Production "Poem"

Do I have to sit and watch
television 23 hours or 24?
Can't I look out of the window
and see the trees, sit on my own lawn
without getting wet,
attacked, ignored, or feeling guilty?
Am I a prisoner in my own house?
Have I got a roof over my head
a floor beneath my feet
do I have arms, to touch you
legs to walk on —
eyes to see the world as it is?
Is everything folding up, ending, gone?
To be human do I have to
have short hair, wear a tie
go to nightclubs
dance to jazz tunes
fifty years old?
Do I have to drink cheap
champagne
to be anyone?
If I don't buy a lottery ticket
have I got a chance
to become rich —
powerful, wealthy?
Can I read books

nobody is ready to read
and still be knowledgeable
well-informed — about my time?
Am I hopelessly retarded?
Will I look like a decent person
if I wear a beard?
Am I allowed to have a dog
a cat — a monkey, an iguana
and be rejected by the young and the dutiful?
Did I hear birds sing in my ear — or am I hearing things?

Can I experiment in prose
and still be greeted
by my neighbor —
Am I the only one left
at the table when the others
have all gone to listen
to the visiting psychiatrist
lecture about
unreasonable acts
of non-profitable living!
Can I still walk down the avenues
fron the Oakland Hills
Berkeley, Hayward to
Saint Bernardino — and
still call myself a poet?

If I don't
read the newspaper
for a single morning
will I be aware of what the
northern hemisphere's up to?
Will I miss anything
if I don't go to a movie
three times a week!
Can I still be meek without
being arrogant or silly?
Can I still carry on a lively
conversation over my shoulder
without hanging my head in shame?
Are Afghanistan, Nicaragua, the Middle East, Tibet,
Cuba, El Salvador, zones still open to
my way of thinking?
Am I supposed to say yes
to all the insults, refusals,
the rejections, the put-downs,
the affronts, the snubs, the
cold shoulders?
Will I ever find a woman
who will agree with me on something —
Was I really born in the 20th century?

1985

Mon Nom De Plume

Cities crawl into each other like frightened
animals: bats or rats? Silvery vistas
replace reptilian roads winding into
nowhere; the vague outer darkness blushing
no permits issued to become a woman
for the night; permanent displacements
of speech uttered by the same bland
characters in luxurious apartments
they can't afford; the tone crumbles
as it comes out of the mouth: on the
floor a hysterical woman in a fit
writhes; she is offered a snake but
she obviously is not aware of it; much
spilling of noise over the loudspeakers.
Crackling: pictorial fragments of cheering
roaring automobiles — surging waves,
crowds and the silence of distant storm lit by
patches of clear light; below the
waiter opens a bottle while the old peasant
offers his praises to the Lord; I too
praise the inexistant Lord for having
allowed me to exist and read the
Chants of Maldoror written by I.D.
under the N.D.P. Comte de Lautréamont.

DANIEL MOORE

The Heart Looks Out
Across Montana

The heart looks out across Montana,
   gazes out across grassy plains.

Heart's light-beams criss-cross oceans.
Watery creases fold over and over.

The heart's gaze returns
to its point of departure.

The heart in its dome,
the heart in its crystal,
the heart in its delirium,
of sensing and encompassing, held in a glory,
delighting in suspension,
hangs in its flight
    above everything at once.

Is an opening to what was,
what is, and a
funnel of what's to come
in one blink of its systole/diastole wing-beat
without leaving its
     place.

Everything else falls away.
It goes where it goes.

Spins in its orbit.
Balancing gyroscope.
Calls to us
   as our
      intelligent navigator.

Contains the whole universe more than
the universe contains it —

undimensional heart.

The Wait

While I'm waiting a half hour for the
    next train, having missed the one I
walked like a startled ostrich to miss, through the
    gently rainy bright green May Philadelphia
10:30 AM streets to the station, past
      banks of irises both pale and bright,

I could sit here on the broken wooden
fleck-painted bench and write

the entire history of the world, heartbeat by
    heartbeat! The outcome and
      origin of all our
        striving, a loving eyewink at the right time, or the
flat of an oppressive hand against a
    bare baby buttock that started our
uprise or downfall through all the
    tangled years of our lives —

I could write prehistoric mudholes, futuristic vertigos —

The great ones on their deathbeds, some of them
    afraid and drooling,
      yellow eyes rolling in their
    dry heads as they watch death's angel
      bend close, blowing ever so slightly those
        unsightly misty blue breaths, puff! puff!
Or else the deathbed scenarios of
    the great ones who grow solemn — eternity fills their
      mouths with its light golden marbles, and
        each serene word comes out
          round.

I could sit here facing the parallel tracks in the rain and solve
in a flash
the inexorable mysteries of mathematics! Numbers
    never converge, they run on parallel tracks, disappear
        at last into the One! Appear again like
        slick acrobats, ready to do their
anti-gravitational turns —

I could sit on this bench and see in my mind's eye
    the start of all the
    biological processes that
      got me here,
the tiny illuminated radiolaria, fragile
gelatinous spokes of the determined wheel of
    light enerized with the
same smooth music that keeps planets like
        Neptune in black space spinning —

I could, in the time left before the
    train comes, write the
history of history, as well as all
    literature and wisdom — that
    single dot of God-sent bright light that
burns through the pages of every book ever written,
every book opened and read, that white heat of
    spirit-force and the
      relentless forward movement of
        ingenious thought over the
        arid plains of
paper and ink into the
    torn breast of each reader —

I could decipher the
    equipoise mechanism of language, that
both sun and moon reflect on the tongue's moisture
and send burning and icy beams of love through every
communication, by dolphin, dog, or

man, insect, mite or
minister —

I could sit here and write all the
mortal nights and days left to us, the Titanics of
civilizations sunk to the bottom, Utopias
risen on stilts above the
muck of despair and longing
only to topple through the rise of the human ego
mushrooming in a perfect place with
the usual blood-lust for
perfect power —

I could unweave the mystical labyrinths of sex,
that coiled green drive that opens out
velvety buds of lavender in which green
neon snakes linger and strike,
coil and intercoil of slippery
gleam-grease, flutterings and
upturned spouts and
inturned cisterns where
a liquid like slick sound
slithers over our
bodies like
a blue soap —

Or I could resolve all the tragedies of love, have
Romeo and Juliet not die, but
open their slow eyes in that
cobwebby crypt and glance
over to each other from their
biers and their
eyes fill with
tears and their
mouths make sounds only
their own ears
hear.

Ecstasies and contemplative loop-the-loops! The vast and cratered
   history of the heart!
Bodily farewells and the souls' entertainments! Laying back and
    basking in
      God's Light. Arrivals in full
        regalia, stark naked!
Samothrace, that headless statue, with white wings flung wide
    and her head miraculously
        on again, smiling!
The joy of God's encirclement!
      The long glass trumpets of His
        Greeting! The
endless dunes of His breathy Silences
    throughout the worlds! God's Voice
      like a perfect word, ending in a
        Shout!
  Everything and nothing! At the
      heart of all our
        befuddlement —
  Zone opened suddenly, going
      nowhere and everywhere, at once!

All this, as I sit here, in this
   ramshackle train-station (Tolstoy could have
      died here!), rain
        glistening down in strings
    dangling in front of me,
      twinkling on the
straight tracks, waiting here
    for the train!

5/20

PHILIP M. KLASKY

original fire

after swimming in the lake
blue water in desert
after swimming in the stinging salt and sea dust
white chalk covers my body
except in the rings around my neck
ochre lines of sweat
underarm, along the inside of my thighs

a cloud of black and white pelicans
beats the sky,
the ancient birds scatter the sand across the beaches
pyramid emerging from the center of the lake
covered with spider webs
ringed by volcanic water
mixing quickly with the night cool

we were watching the storm all day
thunderheads sliced by sunlight
clawhammer hits steel
I lie down on top of you
and cover your body with my chalk caked skin
the sun heats the sand
calling to the glass
we draw patterns on our bodies
a cloud releases a strike of lightning
begged by the ground
draped in thunder
the bolt shatters a pine tree into flame

you grab the blanket and run away from the flash
wings trailing behind you
you dance zigzag through sagebrush
toward the truck
like the small girl
watching the neighbor's farmhouse burn to the ground
animals flee from the barn
horses pitch over the fence,
chickens burst through the yard

and I run toward the flaming tree
excited to gather a piece of original fire

MARC PETRIE

3 POEMS

L.A. Pantry

I suspect the frescoes.

Byzantine buildings harbor cigar smoke and maniacs.
Madman rants "No heaven. I don't care what that preacher says."
A bored doorman spits on the sidewalk.
There are lots of fountains in this part of town — you
practically trip over them between the destitute —
imagistic fountains, the skeletons of the city,
planted rocks and irrigated stream beds,
fountains in slim channels pouring over rock walls,
water rechanneling itself,
this is a chamber of commerce kind of day.

I am at the Pantry before I know it —
hardly a wait for the counter.
I order an eight-ounce club steak and dig into
the cole slaw and bread, get grease on my notebook.
I wait for rejection slips in my mail.
I live for failure.
This certainly increases my appetite. I am
famished.

Always eat a steak like it's your last meal.

This steak is so good. Sure real meat. Charred outside,
pink inside. I plop steak sauce. I cut into it and enjoy it with my
    tooth and mouth,

gulp it down my deep voice, associate it with all that lives in the lost
    world inside
my stomach.

In the meantime, I muse over the straight talk of coffee
steaming in my cup — but the grease spot on my new shirt
is nothing to be read and sung about. In the absence of field
this city lights its avenues with people and distant sun.

Ah, that was good.

I will put my tip on the counter and walk back out into the wild and
    passionate
world I make home, dark inside my own paranoia.

Let the dice roll as they may

Wipe Out

My father died two weeks ago.
I've surfed every day since.
I try to wash away my grief
in salt-water baths, in sessions
from Santa Cruz to San Diego;
at O 'Neil's, at 41st St, at Gaviota,
at the Santa Ana River Jetty, at Blackie's,
at Brooks Street, at Sano, at Old Man's,
at Tamarack, at Ponto, at Swami's;
at all the old haunts where I've ridden
early morning breakers watching the dawn patrol
pelicans and where I've spent lonely evenings
watching the sunset, trying to piece it all together.
I paddle out with heavier arms and heavy heart each day.
Each session sucks my energy and leaves nothing but
fatigue and sorrow.

I'm driving south on P.C.H. down past Seal Beach and I notice big
  peaks; the sea
froths in crested buttes
six to seven feet so I pull into the state park and drive to the south
  end — that's
where the best summer surf is on this beach.
I study the currents from my car-they flow hard to the south.
I decide to get wet anyway.
I need something large in my life.
I point my mini-tank northwest,
its nose plows the seas,
water sprays back onto my face
I keep paddling, duck-dive with little enthusiasm
and less precision. I bob like a cork too fast
and find myself caught in the soup.
I can't get beyond the soup.
I am nearly to Huntington
and my arms are too tired to fight
and my mind is too weary to comprehend
The sixty-eight degree water seems cold
and I wished I had worn a wet suit.
After 15 minutes I cannot remember my father
in the struggle I decide to ride an insider,
to call it a day, to rest tomorrow.
It's walled out.
I make a bad decision
on a four foot wall that crashing
I get my hands on the rails and hop up
but the board slips out from under me
while the face caves in and throws me forward.
I know I am in trouble because I am falling
in the direction that the board will come
and, sure enough,
the board rides up over me —
the skag plows my back;
it carves a deep furrow
from my kidney to my shoulder
then bangs against the base of my skull.

The impact pushes me down and I am caught under
the turbulent mass of white water that
turns me as if I went over the falls in a barrel
and my leash pulls at my ankle and flips my leg
up to where my head should be.
I do not know where the surface is anymore.
It is quiet here.
The liquid fills my ears,
salt water runs up my nostrils
and begins to fill my sinuses,
I begin to gag.
I let the last air bubbles escape.
No surface noise, not the crash of waves,
not the wind whistling off my board,
not the cries of the sea birds swirling overhead
reach me here, beneath the surface.
I have known brutality like this before on the surface
but this force leaves me numb.
My grief overrides my desire to fight.
For a moment, I consider letting the water wash clean
whatever I have left inside
so that I may remain in this silent world.
Panic sets in.
I shake my head fast.
I shake off the wooziness.
I break the silent fast
with my arms pulling like propellers
and kick off the sandy bottom
to push up like polaris
I penetrate the liquid skin —
I reach the surface to fight
the tides and the currents and the noise and the light.
I pull my board which flounders in the soup
I take in air — a sharp pain shocks the air when it reaches
salt water in my lungs and sinuses.
I get hold of my board and
belly up onto it like a seal
I steer it to the shore.

I am too tired to stand.
I roll off it and force myself to my knees
then throw up salt water on the sand
before I rise on shaky legs.
My back stings where the salt water
has entered the gash.
I shiver and shake across the sand
then re-enter the real world where my pain remains with me.
I change in dry shorts, t-shirt, drive home, then to the hospital.
I have walked out of the sea
      an ancient fish,
          a new species,
              a missing link
to a new world I want to recover.

Palm Sunday

Walking around the Orange traffic circle that flows through my
    desert heart,
looking at the neon woodpecker hollow red beak, angry red eyes,
    blue crown on empty head,
floating down the streets of the sea of Los as I wait for Angels,
finding myself thinking how I would like to leave Los Angeles like a
    bad dream,
watching the road peel away from the green hills of spring and the
    white peaks of San Bernardino,
spacing my response to the smiles of strangers who are fellow
    travelers on this train,
questions arise like dust in the desert.

Did Nixon win the war on fags,
Did Reagan bring dishonor in pieces,
Did Bush buy Barbara at a Moroccan slave market,
Does the coastal Berber culture differ from the Mauritanian,
Does Paul Bowles know both cultures, know neither, or how to
    make a good cup of tea while he chops mint,
Does the Vintage collection of Modern American Poetry really
    contain no work by either Bukowski or Kerouac,
Does a woman's face give me a glimpse into heaven under golden
    hair flipping, downcast eyes, inert exposed sensuality blowing
    out of her self and bouncing off her aura rubbing up against
    mine,
In heaven, are there flat, green plains and stands of pine trees I can
    rest under,
can I heal myself,
can I find the bad times I play hide-and-seek with, tap them on the
    shoulder, make them IT so they can no longer hide,
can I watch the moon turning from quarter to half to full and see
    my soul, see my soul as it was before I came to be, see my soul
    as a willing occupant of this body, see my soul as happy to be
    born of flesh and enter this world, see my soul as happy, lose
    the pain wrapped like a cancer around my heart and be happy,

loose the rosaries chained around my ankles and leap from this
    canyon,
can I watch the moon and be happy,
can I watch the moon and be happy,
can I watch the moon and be happy,
can I dance on the head of a pin,
can I dance on the head of a pin with all the others who share my
    pain,
can I hold hands with them and skip to the harmonium as joy
    echoes across the hills,
will daddy shove spanish bayonet through my stomach,
will my glass ego shatter into a million pieces,
will I be able to love my wife,
will I be able to lose my suspicion like a loud sports coat,
is Ross happy, is Ross really dead,
Is it possible to find peace and happiness in death as it is not in life,
do daddies beat you after you die?
These questions fall onto the rocks that line the stony desert like
    corpses on the slag heap.
The ocotillo is in bloom.
It must have rained recently. I take one red long honeysuckle
    blossom from the ocotillo and put it in my shirt pocket to
    carry with me.

I see a road runner on a field mixed with desert and human
    garbage. I follow it where it leads me. It leads me to a culvert
    then walks away.
There, under a greasewood tree, I see a purple cactus blossom. I
    almost miss it in my rush. I walk down the culvert and look
    closer. There are four purple blossoms blooming in the cactus.
    Insects work quietly in each. Each blossom is a separate, active
    universe of its own.
I see a red and white flowered pattern coach abandoned under a
    willow tree next to the culvert. I sit there and wait.
Christ rides out of the wilderness on an ass across the desert rocks
    on this road into Desert Hot Springs. His face is like Ross,'
    like Ross when I would walk him and he leaned his face on my
    shoulder, the simple, soft smile of peace that an angel has after

he is touched by death.

Christ stops under the willow. He dismounts and walks over. His cheap robe is brown from desert dust. He sits with me on this couch. I give him my offering; a cold can of coke and a palm frond.

We walk over to the giant cholla. We stab our palms and feet with cholla spines to endure the pain we will return to. We walk with bloodied feet to look at the cactus blossom. We smell the purple sacred heart of the palm flower.

He rides off to calvary. I walk back up the road to where the ATMs bloom and burger grease fills the air.

We hold the sacred moment between us.

He rides off on the back of an ass toward the holy city. I drive off to Los Angeles, the unholy, unfulfilled holy city.

LAWRENCE FERLINGHETTI

WORK-IN-PROGRESS

Wearing Apollinaire's derby I am in a zeppelin with a hundred dignitaries in tailcoats from all over the world cruising about looking for a place to declare peace looking for a soft landing for peace on earth Gardens are sighted on the horizon and the airship veers in that direction only to discover there is no airfield and we veer off again The sky is lit with flares A man in tails with wings jumps off the Eiffel tower thinking he's a bird He plummets straight down in front of his friends I am picking petals off a sunflower in Provence It's midsummer A million crickets sound their huge drone in the night A sunflower leans in a window where I am a boy leaning out *Loulou Loulou* someone calls I have picked all the petals They fall *Loulou Loulou Où es-tu* It is hot in the dark room There are riots in France and Italy The Americans killed Sacco and Vanzetti I saw Lindbergh land The zeppelin sails on There is jazz on the radio It's Sidney Bechet Paris 1930s the dignitaries toasting each other in champagne and American cigarettes The pilot sends a Morse code greeting to a ship at sea The band plays on The Captain sends back a round of drinks on the house sailing through the hot night an endless flight around the world We gaze out the portals of the crystal gondola at the endless stars Night reveals the cities of earth lit with leftover sun I am kneeling in short pants in a cathedral somewhere in France Christ died on Friday and rose on Sunday setting a world altitude record out of sight in the dark firmament I don't believe a word of it The wine doesn't taste like blood The dirigible soars in the summit of heaven Where will it ever land The eternal pilot pours over the charts The dawn is pointing On a lake far below the wood boats knock together Life sails on I am stretched out in a sailing-canoe in upstate New York An eagle soars in the summit of heaven An opera hat lies on a marble table in the lobby of the Paris opera High over the city a plane searches the sky making a sound like a gnat It's a plane it's a bird There is a thrill in the air We are walking down the Avenue de l'Opéra The Metro entrance yawns with its art-deco mouth and swallows us The zeppelin flies on into the twenty-first century The zeppelin is life itself The zone we fly through endless without borders without boundaries There are no more nations Migrant hordes sweep the earth in search of food and shelter We throw down our champagne glasses The tv shows the endless night sky We are watching an eclipse The universe endless stretches away in the night There must be a place where all is light Where then O Endless One in endless eternity Where now We are heavenly bodies rapt in time hurtling through bent space Flame-outs illuminate the landscape

DOCUMENTS

D.H. LAWRENCE'S
PAINTINGS AND THE
ELGIN MARBLES

Melina Mercouri, who died March 6, 1994, was not the only Greek who tried to get the British Museum to return the Elgin Marbles to her country (from whence they had been spirited by Lord Elgin in the early 1880s). Saki Karavas, the owner of ten paintings by D.H. Lawrence in Taos, New Mexico, a few years ago offered to return the paintings to England if the Elgin Marbles were returned to Greece.

But the story begins much earlier. The paintings (innocuous sylvan scenes in which clunky nudes seem about to think about caressing each other) were exhibited at the Warren Galleries in London in 1929 and were seized as obscene by Scotland Yard but later released to Lawrence on the condition he never exhibit them in England again. He took them to Taos shortly thereafter, and there they remain for all to see in the office of Mr. Karavas, the owner of Hotel La Fonda.

Also to be seen on his walls are the original letters he wrote to the British government and the replies he received, as well as one from Lawrence's literary executor, Laurence Pollinger. Although the Leader of the Opposition in the House of Commons did not leap at the exchange of marbles for paintings, the Home Secretary did intimate that, given the slight shift of contemporary attitudes, British Customs might indeed not seize them again were they to be returned to merry England. The letters are here reproduced for the first time.

Telephone **GERRARD 7088**
Telegrams **HIPOL WESDO**
LONDON
Cables **HIPOL, LONDON**

PEARN, POLLINGER & HIGHAM, Ltd.

Authors Agents

76, DEAN STREET, SOHO,

LONDON, W.1.

New York:
DAVID KINDAR
LAURENCE POLLINGER *Managing*

JEAN LEROY
GERALD POLLINGER
MONICA PRETTER
PAUL SCOTT

AIRLETTER   7th January, 1958.

Saki Karavas, Esq.,
Hotel La Fonda de Taos,
Taos,
New Mexico, U.S.A.

Dear Mr. Saki Karavas,

<u>D. H. Lawrence.</u>

Many thanks for your letter of 19th December. Under
Mrs. Frieda Lawrence's Last Will I am appointed Literary
Executor.

I note you have acquired the paintings of D. H. Lawrence,
which were held by Mrs. Lawrence, and that you plan to dispose
of these either as a collection or singly.

I am sorry, but I can think of no possible purchasers in
England, quite apart from the difference between prices that
might be obtainable in the U.S.A. and here. It is true that
London is still a great mart for old masters, and objets d'art,
but not, I should have thought, for D. H. Lawrence's paintings.
There is another point that I think you should bear in mind, and
that is D. H. Lawrence gave an undertaking to the authorities
here that the paintings would never come back to this country.
It was, if my memory serves, on these conditions that Scotland
Yard and the Home Office returned the paintings to D. H. Lawrence
after they had seized and closed down the exhibition of them
here.

I shall look forward to seeing and talking with you upon
your visit to London next month.

Yours sincerely,

LP/MD.

3 August 1976

Dear Mr. Kasoors

Thank you for your letter of 3rd July about paintings by
D. H. Lawrence which you have in your collection.

I do not think it is right to say that Lawrence's paintings
were ever banned from England. What you may have in mind is that
in 1929 proceedings were taken in respect of thirteen particular
paintings which formed part of an exhibition of Lawrence's work
arranged at the Warren Galleries in London, it being alleged that
those paintings were obscene. The issue of their obscenity was
not finally determined by the court, because by a compromise the
paintings were handed back on receipt of an undertaking that they
would not be further exhibited.

As Home Secretary I have no power to interfere with the
institution of proceedings in individual cases and cannot therefore
give any undertakings about whether or not particular works would
be likely to give rise to future proceedings; but the law which I
introduced in 1959 enables articles which are alleged to be obscene
to be defended on the grounds of their artistic merit. In any
event, it is undoubtedly true that the changes in attitudes to
which you refer have been reflected in the adjudications of the
English courts.

The importation of paintings into the United Kingdom would be
subject to the separate controls of the Customs and Excise Acts,
which prohibit the import of indecent or obscene articles. Again,
I have no responsibility for the operation of these controls and
it will be for customs officers to decide on the merits at the
time of importation whether in the light of current law and
contemporary attitudes particular articles are to be regarded as
falling within the prohibition.

Yours sincerely,

Roy Jenkins

SAKI KARAVAS
TAOS, NEW MEXICO 87571
(505) 758-2211

The Rt.Hon. Neil G. Kinnock, M.P.
The House of Commons
Westminsiter, London, S.W.I.

Dear Mr Kinnock :

I believe I am correct in recalling that you made a statement
some years ago that you would act to restore the Elgin Marbles to
Greece in the event that a parliamentary majority of your party
raised you to the position of first lord of the treasury and
prime minister. My recollection is that Melina Mercouri was in
London at the time seeking support for the return of the Marbles.

The purpose of my letter is to suggest that in the likely
event that you become head of H. M. Government and indeed move to
return the Marbles, I would like to show my gratitude by returning to Great Britain the important paintings, ten in all, that
were done by D.H. Lawrence and which are now in my possession. I
have had a request from the University of Nottingham asking for
the pictures that were banned in 1929 by Scotland Yard when they
were exhibited at the Warren Galleries in London. Technically,
despite the obvious change in the public attitude towards what
was then considered obscene, the pictures could perhaps still be
detained by H. M. Customs & Excise. Lawrence was able to retrieve
his pictures when he assured the police that they would not be
shown in England.

All of this now seems to be a bit of antiquarian history. I
have owned the pictures since the death of Lawrence's widow and
have naturally had several offers to purchase them. This letter,
which goes with my best wishes for your success in the next
general elections, perhaps suggests an odd quid pro quo. But I
would be happy to have your opinion of it and also some further
indication of your feeling about the Elgin Marbles and their
future.

Sincerely,

Saki Karavas

154

HOUSE OF COMMONS
LONDON SW1A 0AA

The Office of the

Leader of The Opposition

February 5th 1990

Dear Saki Karavas,

Mr Kinnock has asked me to thank you for your
letter about DH Lawrence's paintings. I
apologise for the delay in replying.

Mr Kinnock's views on the Elgin Marbles are
well-known, but he does not regard these
matters as appropriate for "quid pro quo"
bargains. Obviously the return of DH Lawrence's
paintings to Britain would of itself be
interesting and worthwhile.

Yours sincerely,

Charles Clarke
Personal Assistant to Neil Kinnock

Ezra Pound and Pier Paolo Pasolini   Photograph by V.U. Contino

PIER PAOLO PASOLINI

INTERVIEWS

EZRA POUND

Pasolini "Oh let an old man rest."[1]

That's how this Canto ends. I well know, Pound, that I'm here to disturb your rest. But first, I must show you how I feel on meeting you. I'll read something you wrote. Do you remember one of your "Lustra" poems addressed to Walt Whitman? It says: "I make a pact with you, Walt Whitman — I have detested you long enough. I come to you as a grown child who has had a pig-headed father; I am old enough now to make friends. It was you that broke the new wood, now is a time for carving. We have one sap and one root — Let there be commerce between us."[2]

I could read this poem, changing only two little details: your name and one other thing. I'd read it thus: "I make a pact with you *Ezra Pound* — I have detested you long enough. I come to you as a grown child who has had a pig-headed father; I am old enough now to make friends. It was you who began carving, now is the time to break the new wood. We have one sap and one root — let there be commerce between us."

Pound Fine, friends then: *pax tibi, pax mundi.*

Pasolini There's another point I'd like to make. I'd like to ask you brutally how you feel toward European culture, as one who belongs to what you called "οι βαρβαροι," the barbarians? When you came to Gibraltar from America, did you feel like one of these "οι βαρβαροι" arriving in Europe?

Pound	I don't think I had as a young man any inferiority complex. My arrival at Gibraltar in 1908 was not a first visit, but a return. I'd been in Europe as a boy of twelve, as I wrote in "Indiscretions," an autobiographical piece about my early years.
Pasolini	I say this because, after reading your essays — fine literary essays — in spite of their profound erudition and the immense critical acumen they contain, there's something barbarous about them.
Pound	My prose did in fact become crude during a certain period. It was a reaction, perhaps, to mixing with a respectable entourage.
Pasolini	"Eat of it not in the underworld./ See the sun or the moon bless thy eating,/κορη, κορη, for the six seeds of an error,/ or that the stars bless thy eating,/ o Lynx, guard this orchard,/ keep from Demeter's furrow,/ this fruit has a fire within it,/ Pomona, Pomona,/ No glass is clearer than the pomegranate body,/ holding the flame?/ Pomona, Pomona,/ Lynx, keep watch on this orchard / that is named Melagrana,/ or the Pomegranate field,/ The sea is not clearer in azure,/ nor the Heliads bringing light / here are lynxes, here are lynxes,/ Is there a sound in the forest / of pard or of bassarid / or crotale or of leaves moving?/ Cythera, here are the lynxes,/ will the scrub-oak burst into flower?/ There is a rose vine in this underbrush./ Red? White? No, but a colour between them / when the pomegranate is open and the light falls / half through it./ Lynx, beware of these vine-thorns / o Lynx, δλαυχῶπιζ, coming up from the olive yards,/ Kuthera, here are Lynxes and the clicking of crotales / there is a stir of dust from old leaves / will you trade roses for acorns,/ will Lynxes eat thorn leaves?"[3]

I'll read these lines: "Under white clouds, cielo di Pisa,/ out of all this beauty something must come."[4]

Pound	They are good lines.
Pasolini	Yes, very good. Among your best.
Pound	But good lines in my work are sparse. I didn't succeed in putting them in a cosmos.
Pasolini	No, I don't believe that. I think your poetry resembles life. You say your poetry is like speech between intelligent people. It follows a random, casual curve, with some sublime moments and others that are grey. In my view, your poetry follows this arc, so it isn't true that your best verses are not synthesized . . .
Pound	One tries to give them coherence, and one doesn't succeed.
Pasolini	Let one reader say that you did succeed. Do you think this "randomness" means letting beauty give birth to more beauty, on its own?
Pound	You honor me with your trust.
Pasolini	When you write, is your situation similar to that of the surrealists who write? That is, do you let the inspiration, the word, the language, come out almost automatically, or do you write very slowly, weighing one word at a time?
Pound	I missed out on that.
Pasolini	All critics are in agreement that your poetry is enormously vast. It's as if your poems covered the surface of an immense poetic territory. And this is true, one quotation after another . . .
Pound	They're made at random.
Pasolini	What are at random? The criticisms or the quotations?
Pound	They're made at random, they say, but it isn't true. They're music, musical themes that recur.
Pasolini	This critical judgment seems right to me. Your poetry is

enormously vast, but it's a first impression. Reading it better, all the elements that make it so vast in a certain sense become smaller. For example, to a reader like me, who's unfamiliar with Chinese literature and wisdom, all the Chinese quotations become *flatus vocis,* which are reduced to one element. The same for the Provençal poets' citations, or the Italian *dolce stil novo* poets, and so on, they too are reduced to just one element. While at first your poetry seems to cover a vast territory, gradually, however, it gets deeper. Instead of imagining you spreading over a vast linguistic territory, I see you at the bottom of a well in which you've reduced the world to a few elements: a group of citations that are always the same, a group of friends who return and are always the same, Yeats, Eliot. . . . I see you at the bottom of this narrow well in which you look back and reflect on your life.

Pound   You're going deep and it's hard to reply from the surface where I am now.

Pasolini "In 'The Spring and Autumn' there are no righteous wars."[5] And then: "Why wars? Said the sergeant rum-runner. Too many people, when they're too many, you must kill a few of them." They're pacifist verses. Would you like to take part in one of those demonstrations for peace that happen in America or in Italy?

Pound   I believe in the good intentions, but not in the usefulness of these demonstrations. I look from another viewpoint, as I wrote in an unfinished Canto: "When one's friends hate each other, how can there be peace in the world?"[6]

Pasolini What's the meaning of these lines I quoted: "In *The Spring and Autumn* there are no righteous wars." What is the meaning of *The Spring and Autumn*?

Pound   They're the wings, they are memories, history transmitted.

Pasolini	*The Spring and Autumn* is the title of a Chinese book? In the Chinese tradition?
Pound	Yes. *The Spring and Autumn* is a book attributed by some to Confucius, who was notoriously anything but a warmonger.
Pasolini	You've never been to China?
Pound	No.
Pasolini	Do you regret, in your life, to have never seen China, which has so inspired you?
Pound	Yes, I'd always hoped to see China. It's too late now, who knows . . .
Pasolini	Confucius is one of the names that recur frequently in your poetry. I want to ask you this question, which is a problem for me: Confucius is basically the only religious reformer, the only great religious philosopher who wasn't religious. His philosophy was above all practical, almost secular. I'd like to know how Confucius comes into your poetic world, which, though very secular in its cadence, is enormously religious in its irrationality, in its undecipherability.
Pound	Perhaps I'd have tried to see the Confucian universe as a series of tensions.
Pasolini	One of the innumerable elements that make up the Cantos but are in reality reduced to a small territory at the bottom of this well where you reassess your life, one of these elements is Italy. What appealed to you most at first? The landscape or the people?
Pound	The old landscape is ruined by these roads, where earth is changed for asphalt.
Pasolini	Italy at that time was still preindustrial, agrarian, artisan. Today it's a nation that is largely industrialized, so it produces literary phenomena analogous to those that America or England produced in those times. Italy is

now one of these industrialized nations, which are culturally advanced, and therefore is creating a new kind of literature typical of industrialized, bourgeois nations. In Italy there's a sort of avant-garde movement that often uses your name. Do you accept paternity for these movements?

Pound   You speak of industrialized, and therefore culturally advanced nations. It's that "therefore" I don't accept.

It's difficult for me to reply to your question, because not only in an industrialized Italy has there been a great increase, as you yourself say, of these neo-avant-garde products, but throughout the world, and it's impossible for me to keep up to date or, I was about to say, to keep afloat.

Pasolini Are you pleased that your name is used by the maker of these Italian neo-avant-garde products, or not?

Pound   If your theory of the old exile down in the dark well, reassessing his past life, is exact — I don't agree, yet maybe you are right — I wouldn't be in the position to see clearly what's happening outside, under the neon lights of the neo-world of the neo-avant-gardists, who I hope will understand and forgive those who can't see them.

Pasolini Who are the painters you liked most?

Pound   I think those of the quatrocento.

Pasolini And among your contemporaries? Those who were working from '17 to '30, when you were young?

Pound   Léger.

Pasolini Did you like most the painters whose work resembled your poetry, or painters who belonged to a different world?

Pound   I once wrote in the margins of a letter to the painter Wyndham Lewis: "I'm not very interested in painters."

	In fact, one critic wrote of me: "Pound chooses music and sculpture to compare them to poetry and has never shown a special interest in painting."
Pasolini	The second of your Pisan Cantos begins thus: "Out of Phlegethon,/ out of Phlegethon,/ Gerhart / are thou come forth out of Phlegethon?/ With Buxtehude and Klages in your satchel, with the / Ständebuch of Sachs in your luggage / — not of one bird but of many."[7] Here the poem stops and a musical score follows.
Pound	There were the first bars of this score, not the rest. There's too much.
Pasolini	What music is it?
Pound	This "Song of the Birds" is by Jannequin, written for a choir. Francesco da Milano transcribed it for lute and Gherard retranscribed it for violin.
Pasolini	I'll read two verses which, I believe, concern your life. You wrote them in the Pisan Cantos, at a moment that was very painful in your life. "The young Dumas weeps because the young Dumas has tears."[8] Did you think of yourself as the "young Dumas"?
Pound	No, with "the young Dumas" I was not thinking of myself. Indeed, in one of the Pisan Cantos I wrote: "*Tard, très tard je t'ai connue, la tristesse*" (Late, too late I met you, sadness).[9]
Pasolini	"What thou lov'st well shall not be reft from thee,/ what thou lov'st well is thy true heritage,/ whose world, or mine or theirs/ or is it of none?/ First came the seen, then the palpable/ Elysium, though it were in the halls of hell,/ what thou lovest well is thy true heritage / pull down thy vanity, it is not man / made courage, or made order, or made grace,/ pull down thy vanity, I say pull down / learn of the green world what can be thy place,/ in scaled invention or true artistry,/ pull down thy vanity, Pasquin, pull down!/ The green casque has

outdone your elegance./ "Master thyself, then others shall thee beare."/ Pull down thy vanity / Thou art a beaten dog beneath the hail,/ a swollen magpie in a fitful sun,/ half black half white,/ nor knowst'ou wing from tail / pull down thy vanity / how mean thy hates / fostered in falsity,/ pull down thy vanity / rathe to destroy, niggard in charity,/ pull down thy vanity,/I say pull down!/ But to have done instead of not doing/ this is not vanity./ To have, with decency, knocked that a Blunt should open,/ to have gathered from the air a live tradition,/ or from a fine old eye the unconquered flame,/ this is not vanity./ Here error is all in the not done,/ all in the diffidence that faltered."[10]

[1] E. Pound, "Cantos," (The Pisan Cantos) LXXXIII.
[2] E. Pound, "A Pact," (in "Lustra," 1926).
[3] E. Pound, "Cantos," (The Pisan Cantos) LXXIX.
[4] E. Pound, "Cantos," (The Pisan Cantos) LXXXIV.
[5] E. Pound, "Cantos," (The Pisan Cantos) LXXVIII.
[6] E. Pound, "Cantos," from CXV.
[7] E. Pound, "Cantos," (The Pisan Cantos) LXXV.
[8] E. Pound, "Cantos," (The Pisan Cantos) LXXX.
[9] E. Pound, "Cantos," (The Pisan Cantos) LXXX.
[10] E. Pound, "Cantos," (The Pisan Cantos) LXXXI.

This interview took place in the fall of 1967 and was broadcast by RAI on June 19, 1968 in a program directed by Vanni Ronsisvalle, "An Hour with Ezra Pound." Quotations from Pound's *Cantos*, courtesy of New Directions.

ARTHUR RIMBAUD

LETTER TO THE AMERICAN NAVY

Bremen, the 14 maj 77

The undersigned Arthur Rimbaud — Born in charleville (France) — Aged 23 — 5 ft 6. height — Goodhealthy, — late a teacher of sciences and languages — Recently deserted from the 47? Regiment of the French army, — Actually in Bremen without any means, the French Consul refusing any Relief, —

Would like to Know on which conditions he could conclude an immediate engagement in the American navy.

Speaks and writes English, German, French, Italian and Spanish.

Has been four months as a sailor in a Scotch bark, from Java to Queenstown. from August to December 76.

Would be very honoured and grateful to receive an answer.

John Arthur Rimbaud

ALLEN TOBIAS

REMEMBERING CARL SOLOMON:
Writer, Editor, Inspiration, Friend

I want to say how I first met Carl, and something about my slight and on-again off-again friendship with him and how it came to be special to me. Once upon a time, Carl Solomon was known to me only through a poem. I knew Carl through Allen Ginsberg, whose "Howl" I've admired since a day when a boy passed a copy of a small book through an opening in the locked gate of our high school. I'm not quite sure that I read "Howl for Carl Solomon" back then. But I understood the defiance and liberation of it; I hid my copy in a back pocket: Ferlinghetti didn't name these the City Lights "Pocket Poets Series" for nothing, you know. But a great poem is only a poem.

I discovered "Howl" in 1958. Later, I came to know Allen better, but Carl eluded me. He remained for me still only a literary persona until the moment I "disappeared" myself from poetic life and threw my body into the nightshift at a Ford Motor plant, a place raining fire, and where I lasted less than three years.

One day, as was my daily habit going to work, I ascended the subway into a maze of overpasses and footbridges, and entered a wide-open terminal sunk between two pillars. These anchored the George Washington Bridge on its Manhattan side. Dozens of men stood directly below me, queuing out along a ramp of the bridge and waiting a ride to the plant. That terminal, a vast space, made each traveller feel and dread his own soul's presence there. And there, beyond the nut shop that floated up at the center of the place, was one single element of peace, something resembling ordinary, orderly life: at the south east corner of the arcade was a lone book shop.

It was 1971 or '72 or '73. I had given up my habit of reading, except for those books dressed in red jackets made in China. But here, in this place full of the familiar smell and touch of books, I tast-

166

ed crumpled pages, and my devoted learning rose up, calling to me. I got beyond my dreariness, to sprawl and dream. Here was a man, dressed in a shabby suit, a lone figure, a cashier perched above me in his booth, intended to spy out shoplifters like myself, and himself in former years. Alone in his presence, I forgot myself. It was an unconscious scene. I gathered words, prepared to renounce my efforts to "proletarianize" myself, and the world.

I more than once stumbled through these aisles. I found myself awake, feverish, and bemused. The likes of Kenneth Rexroth and Kenneth Patchen lived here I knew, and I fastened onto them, in their paperback lives, like old forgotten friends. "The sea is awash with roses," I remembered, "and the land." The clerk was more knowledgeable than I. One day we spoke of Seymour Krim. I admired his title, I said, "the one about a 'Near-Sighted Cannoneer.'" Immediately, I recognized a face. "Aren't you . . . ?" and yes, he was "Carl Solomon." Through my interruptions in which I said how much I'd enjoyed the *Mishaps* books Carl told his history, a broken-down history, and later a history of the miracle of beat publication from his point of view.

In the months since his death I've debated gently concerning Carl's contribution, with those who would listen. Like his selfhood, that contribution was more complex than generally felt. And of course, Carl never drew attention to it. He remained embarrassed about "Howl," a poem written afresh but in a long tradition, going back beyond "Lycidas" and beyond even David's lament for Jonathan: a poem to youth, whose destruction a loving friend cannot prevent. In any case, Allen survived, and yet Carl was not dead. No, he held on. There he was, caged inside the bridge, and me in the auto factory on my political mission!

Carl was then and remained many things: a friend who cared enough to be honest, and a writer and critic of dissenting views. Beginning in the late '40s and '50s he assisted the publication of the avant-guard. In those early days, Carl played a great role, second only to Allen Ginsberg and City Lights in getting the work of his peers read, edited and published. Please read his published works. Carl was a publicist with discernment, with shifting views, and no professional stake in things: his was not noblesse oblige, or cynical detachment, but a privileged madness. More about Carl, whom I hadn't seen in almost twenty years. The years passed, and one day I came as a visitor to Allen Ginsberg's seminar at CUNY grad center. A body I knew passed before me through the classroom door. It wore a familiar blue coat, and sat near me, a big and heavy form. As Allen introduced the class, I pass a note to Carl. "Aren't you Carl?" I wrote. "Yes, of course I am," he nodded. Allen had stumbled onto him, Carl said, in an art gallery, and now was introducing Carl to students, and to a Polish-American reporter from Danzig! When Carl spoke briefly, a certain reserve, his strain or embarrassment, remained.

After, we, Carl and I, went for coffee, and we talked about his poetry and travel, his early marriage, a failure, his rootedness in Judaism, which had revived in each of us. He quoted Rimbaud on "un certain dérangement," a deliberate disordering of the senses, and noted his misgivings about Allen's mission. We then exchanged telephone numbers and agreed we'd meet again. We did talk a few more times on the phone.

Suddenly, I was moving to Cambridge. Carl wrote me about one of my short stories, "Saragasso Sea." On a dark day in winter, I wandered Harvard Square, returning home in the excitement of discovery. "Carl's the author of another book," I told my wife, "and one I hadn't even heard of. I can't believe my luck in finding it." And so I was answering Carl's letter, full of enthusiasm now, to tell him I'd be down for a visit to the Bronx.

We're near the end now since I am visiting Bob Rosenthal this winter and learn that Carl is ill. Perhaps terminally ill! That night I call and speak to Carl, who sounds very weak. It's a pity I must return home. Hope to visit when I am down again. I call next day from Cambridge. No answer, so I call again. I know. Though not confirmed. After days, I get in touch with Bob. Carl is dead. I'm very sad. But glad to know Carl made it to three score and ten. My heroes, like Tennessee Williams, like to live to seventy! What Bob says cheers me, and I thank him.

"He left us doing well" was Bob's report. Friendship and love remained for Carl, in and out of the madhouse, his strong suit. He had a girl-friend now. Not lonely. Draped in an American flag, Carl Solomon, proud beyond measure for his service in the wartime merchant fleet. And of all things, a Jewish burial! What a true blue, stand-up guy you are, Carl, for all your troubles and your wanderings. I will miss you Carl Solomon: for your honesty, openness, opinions and good humor.

A final word. After Carl's death I learned, or read, and disbelieved, that Carl had a biographer. And yet, I hope that this improbable he or she took careful notes. Carl was a most reliable source-witness to the making of post-WW II American poetry. He made it and he understood it his own way, critically, without ado or too much attachment. Carl I hope you are listening. It would have been enough for us that your friendship inspired, partly inspired, inspired less than the title implies, but more than you claim, one of the great lyrical poems of our time. Or that, befriending Allen Ginsberg, your "Mishkin," you kept him from worse mischief, helped him to focus on the real and present, though he was "there with you, in Rockland." Carl, it would have been enough, had you not parted the dark waters of creativity, but only written *Mishaps, Perhaps*, and *More Mishaps*. Your friends remember you. You will be missed.

Read at a Tribute to Solomon at The Poetry Project,
St. Mark's Church, NYC, on June 16, 1993.

WHO'S WHO IN THE REVIEW

ROBERT ANBIAN'S second collection of poems, *Antinostalgia,* was published in 1992 by Ruddy Duck Press. His work showed up most recently in *Oxygen* and the electronic journal, *Rif/t.* He's just completed a novel, *The Glittering Zero,* and threatens to write a hundred "We" poems.

AMIRI BARAKA, poet, playwright, novelist, directed the Black Arts Repertory Theater School in Harlem. He has taught at Columbia, Yale, and San Francisco State University, and he was head of African Studies at SUNY, Stonybrook.

ALBERTO BLANCO is a dynamic young Mexican poet also famous as a musician, translator, artists and art critic. He now makes out in Cuernavaca, Morelos, where he has gone to escape the pollution of Mexico City. His most recent book of poems is *Cuenta de los guías.*

WILLIAM S. BURROUGHS is the famous *hombre invisible* who was not seen at the Town Hall poetry reading in New York on May 19, 1994, sponsored by NYU as a part of its week-long conference on Beat writers. His text in this *Review* is a transcription of his telephone voice from Lawrence, Kansas, as it was heard in Town Hall that night.

ANDREI CODRESCU is a Romanian-American poet, provocateur, and radio commentator for "All Things Considered." His essay in this *CLR* was written for a panel at the American Conservatory Theater in San Francisco on the subject: Is There a Common Mythic Theme in American Culture?

SUSAN ETLINGER is a writer and translator in San Francisco. Her translation of Savinio's *Il Signor Münster* was published by Atlas Press in 1992. She is now translating *Mediterraneo* by the Italian poet Umberto Saaba.

DARIO FO is Italy's master of populist theater, as actor, playwright, and songwriter. He has performed *Mistero buffo,* around the world to an audience of over forty million. In Italy he filled stadiums without playing soccer. Best known in this country for his *Accidental Death of an Anarchist,* he was long refused a visa to the U.S.

BARRY GIFFORD is the author of novels *Wild at Heart, Night People, Arise and Walk,* and co-author with Lawrence Lee of *Jack's Book: An Oral Biography of Jack Kerouac.*

J.T. GILLETT inhabits Ashland, Oregon, where he is still writing his last poem and (not-yet published) novels. He has performed in bars, cafes, and backyards throughout the Pacific Northwest, and produced a poetry-jam-session video chapbook.

ALLEN GINSBERG's latest publications are *Snapshot Poetics, Cosmopolitan Greetings: Poems 1986–1993*, and a CD series from Rhino Records.

HOWARD HART has lived in New York, where he played jazz and was a contributing editor to the *Village Voice*. He has also spent time in Tangiers, Europe, Mexico, and San Francisco. City Miner is the publisher of his *Six Sets: Selected Poems*.

PHILIP M. KLASKY is an environmental activist, writer, dancer, and naturalist who is doing graduate work in Environmental Studies at San Francisco State University.

STEVE KOWIT is the editor of *The Maverick Poets* and the author of the collections *Lurid Confessions* and *Pranks*. *The Portable Poetry-Writing Workshop*, a primer for poets, will be published next year by Tilbury House. He lives in the Southern California backcountry near the Tecate border.

JAMES LAUGHLIN has written many books of poetry, essays, and letters, as well as being the publisher of New Directions Books. He is actually the reincarnation of Catullus.

SUBCOMANDANTE MARCOS is the eloquent masked spokesman for the Zapatista liberation movement.

KAYE MCDONOUGH, long-time San Francisco poet and little-press editor, lives near the Ivy in New Haven, where she is raising a lively boy, Nile Corso. Her book *Zelda* was published by City Lights in 1978.

DANIEL (Abd al-Hayy) MOORE's latest books from Zilzal Press are *Awake as Never Before* and *Some of the Mysteries of the Self*. Director of the Floating Lotus Magic Opera Company in the 1960s in San Francisco, he published *Dawn Visions* and *Burnt Heart* with City Lights Books. Moore became a Muslim in 1969, spent years traveling and living in Sufi communities and now lives in Philadelphia, stamping poems on the wind.

NORMAN NAWROCKI is a Canadian cabaret artist best known for his work with Montreal's "rebel news orchestra," Rhythm Activism. Hundreds of his poems and rants have been set to music, and appear in labor, community, and poor people's publications.

PIER PAOLO PASOLINI is known primarily in the U.S. for his films, certainly one of the most powerful directors of postwar Italy, but he was also an important critic, ideologue, and poet. Born in 1922, he died tragically in 1975.

MARC PETRIE came in over the transom, in a zine-type edition of his poems, with no clue as to his whereabouts.

PINA PICCOLO is a translator and teacher of Italian. She is active in theater and poetry in the San Francisco Bay Area.

JEREMY REED is the brilliant young British poet and essayist whose *Red-Haired Android* (poetry) and his imaginative recreation of Rimbaud's life, *Delirium*, are published by City Lights.

ED SANDERS is a writer, composer, and democratic socialist scholar-activist. His *Hymn to the Rebel Cafe* (poetry) came out last year. His most recent projects are *The New Amazing Grace*, with verses from over 100 American poets; *Cassandra*, a musical drama tracing the life of the Trojan prophetess; and *Chekhov, a Biography in Verse*, which Black Sparrow will publish in 1995.

ALBERTO SAVINIO, born Andrea di Chirico in Athens, Greece, was a playwright, composer, painter, critic, and stage designer. Leonardo Sciascia called him "the most interesting Italian writer between the two wars."

ANDREW SCHELLING is a poet, essayist, Sanscrit scholar and trans-lator. His *Dropping the Bow: Poems from Ancient India* won the 1992 Academy of American Poets Award for translation.

LAURA STORTONI, born in Sicily, raised in Milan, is the author of *The Moon and the Island* (poetry); her translations of Italian Renaissance women poets will be published by Italica Press this year. She teaches at the Museo ItaloAmericano in San Francisco.

MARK TERRILL, born in Berkeley in 1953, is a poet and merchant seaman who has lived in Hamburg, Germany, since 1982.

INGEBORG TEUFFENBACH, was an award-winning poet, writer, author of numerous radio plays, and literary critic. She was an influ-ential figure in Austrian literary and cultural circles, organizing liter-ary symposia and poetry workshops for over 25 years. These are her last three poems, brought to our attention by her son Fritjof Capra, written before she died in 1992.

ALLEN TOBIAS, born in Brooklyn, has worked as a street performer, construction and factory worker and teacher. To honor Carl Solomon with a memorial, he returned to his first love, writing.

NANOS VALAORITIS is a Greek poet, novelist, and essayist who taught for many years at San Francisco State University. City Lights published his *My Afterlife Guaranteed*.

GEORGII VLASENKO will have a collection of his poems, *Marvellous Catastrophe*, published in Moscow this year.

ANNE WALDMAN, dynamic poet-performer, directed the Poetry Project at St. Mark's Church-in-the-Bowery for over ten years, and now leads the Department of Writing and Poetics at the Naropa Institute.

CITY LIGHTS PUBLICATIONS

Eberhardt, Isabelle. DEPARTURES: Selected Writings
Eberhardt, Isabelle. THE OBLIVION SEEKERS
Eidus, Janice. VITO LOVES GERALDINE
Fenollosa, Ernest. CHINESE WRITTEN CHARACTER AS A MEDIUM
     FOR POETRY
Ferlinghetti, L. ed., ENDS & BEGINNINGS (City Lights Review #6)
Ferlinghetti, Lawrence. PICTURES OF THE GONE WORLD
Ferlinghetti, Lawrence. SEVEN DAYS IN NICARAGUA LIBRE
Finley, Karen. SHOCK TREATMENT
Ford, Charles Henri. OUT OF THE LABYRINTH: Selected Poems
Franzen, Cola, transl. POEMS OF ARAB ANDALUSIA
García Lorca, Federico. BARBAROUS NIGHTS: Legends & Plays
García Lorca, Federico. ODE TO WALT WHITMAN & OTHER POEMS
García Lorca, Federico. POEM OF THE DEEP SONG
Gil de Biedma, Jaime. LONGING: SELECTED POEMS
Ginsberg, Allen. HOWL & OTHER POEMS
Ginsberg, Allen. KADDISH & OTHER POEMS
Ginsberg, Allen. REALITY SANDWICHES
Ginsberg, Allen. PLANET NEWS
Ginsberg, Allen. THE FALL OF AMERICA
Ginsberg, Allen. MIND BREATHS
Ginsberg, Allen. PLUTONIAN ODE
Goethe, J. W. von. TALES FOR TRANSFORMATION
Hayton-Keeva, Sally, ed. VALIANT WOMEN IN WAR AND EXILE
Heider, Ulrike. ANARCHISM: Left Right & Green
Herron, Don. THE DASHIELL HAMMETT TOUR: A Guidebook
Herron, Don. THE LITERARY WORLD OF SAN FRANCISCO
Higman, Perry, tr. LOVE POEMS FROM SPAIN AND SPANISH AMERICA
Jaffe, Harold. EROS: ANTI-EROS
Jenkins, Edith. AGAINST A FIELD SINISTER
Katzenberger, Elaine, ed. FIRST WORLD HA HA HA!
Kerouac, Jack. BOOK OF DREAMS
Kerouac, Jack. POMES ALL SIZES
Kerouac, Jack. SCATTERED POEMS
Kerouac, Jack. SCRIPTURE OF THE GOLDEN ETERNITY
Lacarrière, Jacques. THE GNOSTICS
La Duke, Betty. COMPAÑERAS
La Loca. ADVENTURES ON THE ISLE OF ADOLESCENCE
Lamantia, Philip. MEADOWLARK WEST
Laughlin, James. SELECTED POEMS: 1935-1985
Le Brun, Annie. SADE: On the Brink of the Abyss
Lowry, Malcolm. SELECTED POEMS
Mackey, Nathaniel. SCHOOL OF UDHRA
Marcelin, Philippe-Thoby. THE BEAST OF THE HAITIAN HILLS
Masereel, Frans. PASSIONATE JOURNEY
Mayakovsky, Vladimir. LISTEN! EARLY POEMS

Mrabet, Mohammed. THE BOY WHO SET THE FIRE
Mrabet, Mohammed. THE LEMON
Mrabet, Mohammed. LOVE WITH A FEW HAIRS
Mrabet, Mohammed. M'HASHISH
Murguía, A. & B. Paschke, eds. VOLCAN: Poems from Central America
Murillo, Rosario. ANGEL IN THE DELUGE
Paschke, B. & D. Volpendesta, eds. CLAMOR OF INNOCENCE
Pasolini, Pier Paolo. ROMAN POEMS
Pessoa, Fernando. ALWAYS ASTONISHED
Peters, Nancy J., ed. WAR AFTER WAR (City Lights Review #5)
Poe, Edgar Allan. THE UNKNOWN POE
Porta, Antonio. KISSES FROM ANOTHER DREAM
Prévert, Jacques. PAROLES
Purdy, James. THE CANDLES OF YOUR EYES
Purdy, James. IN A SHALLOW GRAVE
Purdy, James. GARMENTS THE LIVING WEAR
Purdy, James. OUT WITH THE STARS
Rachlin, Nahid. MARRIED TO A STRANGER
Rachlin, Nahid. VEILS: SHORT STORIES
Reed, Jeremy. DELIRIUM: An Interpretation of Arthur Rimbaud
Reed, Jeremy. RED-HAIRED ANDROID
Rey Rosa, Rodrigo. THE BEGGAR'S KNIFE
Rey Rosa, Rodrigo. DUST ON HER TONGUE
Rigaud, Milo. SECRETS OF VOODOO
Ruy Sánchez, Alberto. MOGADOR
Saadawi, Nawal El. MEMOIRS OF A WOMAN DOCTOR
Sawyer-Lauçanno, Christopher, tr. THE DESTRUCTION OF THE JAGUAR
Scholder, Amy, ed. CRITICAL CONDITION: Women on the Edge of Violence
Sclauzero, Mariarosa. MARLENE
Serge, Victor. RESISTANCE
Shepard, Sam. MOTEL CHRONICLES
Shepard, Sam. FOOL FOR LOVE & THE SAD LAMENT OF PECOS BILL
Smith, Michael. IT A COME
Snyder, Gary. THE OLD WAYS
Solnit, Rebecca. SECRET EXHIBITION: Six California Artists
Sussler, Betsy, ed. BOMB: INTERVIEWS
Takahashi, Mutsuo. SLEEPING SINNING FALLING
Turyn, Anne, ed. TOP TOP STORIES
Tutuola, Amos. FEATHER WOMAN OF THE JUNGLE
Tutuola, Amos. SIMBI & THE SATYR OF THE DARK JUNGLE
Valaoritis, Nanos. MY AFTERLIFE GUARANTEED
Wilson, Colin. POETRY AND MYSTICISM
Wilson, Peter Lamborn. SACRED DRIFT
Wynne, John. THE OTHER WORLD
Zamora, Daisy. RIVERBED OF MEMORY

PARIS AMERICAN
FREE LIBRARY

Left Bank Facing Notre Dame 37 Rue de la Bucherie
OPEN 7 DAYS A WEEK — NOON TO MIDNIGHT

READING ROOMS FOR NON FICTION
Free use of OED, Encyclopedia Brittanica, typewriter, computer, and a
reference library of 30,000 books.

FREE LENDING LIBRARY FOR FICTION
Free loan of up to four books for up to one month from the
Sylvia Beach Collection

OPEN HOUSE EVERY SUNDAY
3 pm Story Telling for Children   4 pm Afternoon Tea
plus Visits To The
PHOTOGRAPHIC MUSEUM OF THE LOST GENERATION

Kilometer zero Paris.
Where the streets of the world meet the avenues of the mind.

CITY LIGHTS

A Literary Meetingplace Since 1953

Bookselling & Publishing in the great tradition
of independent international bookstores

261 Columbus Avenue (at Kerouac Alley)
San Francisco California 94133
[415] 362-8193 Booksellers   [415] 362-1901 Publishers
Please write for our mail order catalog